CIVIL WAR PRISONS

Edited by
William B. Hesseltine

THE KENT STATE UNIVERSITY PRESS

The contents of this book first appeared in Civil War History
volume 8, number 2, under the general editorship of James I.
Robertson, Jr.
© 1962 by The Kent State University Press, Kent, Ohio 44242
All rights reserved
Library of Congress Catalog Card Number 72-84195
ISBN 978-0-87338-129-1 (paper)
Manufactured in the United States of America

The Library of Congress has cataloged the first printing of this
title as follows:

Hesseltine, William Best, 1902–1963, comp.
    Civil War prisons. [Kent, Ohio] Kent State University
Press [1972, c1962]
    123 p. illus. 24 cm. $1.95

    Originally published as v. 8, no. 2 of Civil War history.
    Includes bibliographic references.

    1. United States—History—Civil war—Prisoners and prisons.
I. Civil War history.   II. Title.
E611.H44   973.7'7   72-84195
    ISBN 0-87338-131-9; 0-87338-129-7 (pbk.)   MARC

Library of Congress   72 [4]

CONTENTS

CIVIL WAR PRISONS—
INTRODUCTION

William B. Hesseltine

The American Civil War left behind it a long list of controversies. For decades after Appomattox old soldiers defended their personal honor and did verbal battle in repelling asperities upon the valor of their regiments. Officers sought reversals of decisions of courts martial, begged redress from Congress, or carried their demands for vindication to the sovereign people assembled at polling places. The right of secession, the military competence of George B. McClellan and Braxton Bragg, the behavior of Benjamin F. Butler in New Orleans, at Bermuda Hundred and Wilmington, Dahlgren's Raid and Fort Pillow, the personal judgment and the administrative wisdom of Jefferson Davis, all received full airing and enlisted bitter partisans and valiant foemen. Even after a century, some of the ancient controversies stir emotions and provoke debate.

Yet no controversy ever evoked such emotions as the mutual recriminations between Northern and Southern partisans over the treatment of prisoners of war. Hardly had the war begun when the first prisoners alleged that their captors mistreated them. Throughout the war the complaints, the charges and counter-charges, and the assertions of criminal intent fed the raging fires of propaganda. To the end of their lives ex-prisoners wrote books or letters-to-the-editor, told their stories to country-store gatherings, appeared before congressional committees, or addressed conventions of veterans to recount their adversities and to point accusing fingers at their cruel and conspiratorial enemy. Eventually quick-change journalists reprinted the alleged reminiscences of prisoners; novelists of varying repute found gory and pornographic material in the prisons; and neophyte historians wrote extended term-papers, dripping with footnotes, to support one or another contender in the undying quarrel.

The serious student who would assay the evidence on the administration of prisons and the treatment of prisoners of war faces serious critical

WILLIAM B. HESSELTINE, *a professor of history at the University of Wisconsin, is one of the most respected scholars in the Civil War field. Among his many volumes on Lincoln and the era of the 1860's is* Civil War Prisons, *published in 1930.* Civil War History *is deeply proud to have him as guest editor for this special issue.*

problems. The facts are not always clear, and even the figures do not always mean what they seem to prove. That soldiers unfortunate enough to fall into the hands of the enemy suffered and died admits of no doubt. The records are inadequate, but the estimates which Adjutant General F. C. Ainsworth gave to James Ford Rhodes in 1903 seem reasonable. General Ainsworth counted 193,743 Northerners and 214,865 Southerners captured and confined. Over 30,000 Union and nearly 26,000 Confederate prisoners died in captivity. Rhodes concluded that over 12 per cent of the captives died in Northern prisons and 15.5 per cent died in the South. In Rhodes' opinion, the superior hospitals, physicians, medicines, and foods of the North should have produced a greater disparity in favor of the Union.

Rhodes' mention of hospitals caused Professor Edward Channing to comment that the proportion of deaths in Confederate prison camps was "not far from that of the soldiers in the Union army from disease." He added the suggestion that the prisoners in Andersonville probably had contracted hookworm. The suggestion could open other speculations. Were the number of wounded prisoners known, or the number of soldiers suffering from camp diseases and battle fatigue at the time of their capture, the picture of suffering and death in prisons might become clearer. Certain it is that the prisoners sent to Andersonville were weak and disease-ridden as a result of their long confinement on Belle Isle in the James River, and that many were sick when they were captured. Most of the deaths in Andersonville came in the months after the serious overcrowding had been relieved by sending all prisoners fit to travel to other prisons. In fact, the prison was, for most of its existence, a vast, poorly organized, and inadequate hospital.

A second factor of which any critical reader needs to be aware is related to the truism that no prisoner loves his jailer. Rarely, indeed, and then only briefly and under special circumstances—such as those at Fort Warren early in the conflict—did a few captors fraternize with their charges. More commonly, the prisoners confined in Northern and Southern prisons regarded the officers and guards who restrained them as immediate personal enemies, and believed that regulations imposed upon them came as a result of innate and fiendish malice. Few inmates of the prison camps recognized or sympathized with the problems of their custodians.

But, let it be said too that the custodians were hardly a lovable lot. Neither North nor South had such a surplus of talent that it could spare first-class soldiers or administrators for prison duties. Southerners lacked experience and skill in administrative matters and provided no system of prison organization. General John H. Winder was provost marshal of Richmond—an onerous task for which he was ill-suited by temperament

—and the Union prisons in Libby and on Belle Isle were only an added burden and harassment. At Andersonville, Captains W. S. Winder and Richard B. Winder found that procurement for prisons did not have a high priority among Confederate needs, and they were never able to obtain adequate equipment or proper subsistence. In the North, the administrative system was somewhat better, yet Lieutenant Colonel William H. Hoffman, a more efficient and competent Commissary General of Prisons, was as much a martinet as John H. Winder. In both North and South the guards were poorly disciplined Home Guards, unfit for more arduous or more responsible service. Captives came into immediate contact with poor personnel and formed their opinions about their captors from the specimens they observed patrolling the prison fences.

Whatever observations they made were colored and distorted by the propaganda to which they had been subjected. The press, pulpits, and hustings of each contestant portrayed the enemy as fiendish, and ascribed only diabolic motives to the opposing leaders. Soldiers and civilians on both sides heard atrocity stories which were intended to warp their judgment. Prisoners in confinement and in varying stages of illness were in no position to make objective judgments. It was easy for them to believe that their jailers deliberately subjected them to hardships.

To some extent, to be sure, they were correct. Not all the rules and regulations imposed upon Union prisoners in the South could reasonably be considered necessary security measures. Certainly, Secretary of War E. M. Stanton ordered Northern prison authorities to reduce food, fuel, shelter, and clothing of prisoners to levels which he and the propagandists of the North contended were parallel to conditions in the South. Much of the suffering in Northern prisons was a direct result of these orders.

In the years after the war, when more moderate judgments might have replaced the distortions of war, two factors worked to perpetuate the prison controversy. First, the politicians kept alive the issue and found prison gore fit coloring for the bloody shirt they waved. Then, veterans of the prison camps found that they had difficulty in getting pensions or establishing claims for injuries and illnesses resulting from their confinement. They wrote numerous memoirs and reminiscences to argue that all Union prisoners were entitled to pensions and care because of their mistreatment by the Confederates. Two voluminous government publications, *The Trial of Henry Wirz* and a House committee report on *Treatment of Prisoners of War by the Rebel Authorities,* not only added an aura of authenticity to Northern charges but also furnished source books from which writers of prison memoirs could refresh and enlarge their recollections. Confederates resentfully replied, reiterating old charges and matching the Yankees story for story. The mounting body of literature resolved no problems.

The critical problems confronting the historian who examines the prisons of the 1860's are demonstrated in the papers in this special issue of *Civil War History*. The special accounts of individual prisoners and specific prisons illustrate how carefully an objective student must tread in separating truth from propaganda, deliberate distortion from misunderstanding, malicious intent from tragic accident. Perhaps, indeed, they also illustrate that the atrocities of the prison camps were only phases of the greater atrocity of war itself.

PRISON LIFE AT ANDERSONVILLE

Ovid Futch

Andersonville prisoners faced an acute problem in the sharp limitation of available means for satisfaction of the innate urge to activity. Absence of facilities for recreation and exercise forced them to use their own resourcefulness in seeking diversion.[1]

After roll call each morning, prison authorities permitted the inmates to do as they pleased, so long as they offered no threat of escape. The issuance of rations was time-consuming for prisoners charged with this duty, but not particularly so for others. A police detail engaged fifty men each day, and a few were detailed for outside work such as cooking, baking, burying the dead, cutting wood, clerking, and nursing in the hospital. But the vast majority had to find ways of occupying themselves.

This task was made easier by the lack of necessities and conveniences, which compelled the prisoners to exert themselves to compensate for deficiencies of all sorts. One of the first tasks facing new arrivals—if they were to have any protection from the elements—was construction of huts or "shebangs." These abodes required constant repairs, and not infrequently prisoners tore down their shelters and rebuilt them in improved style. Shortage of clothing led to consumption of a great deal of time in making and mending clothes. Keeping clean was especially time-consuming, since usually no soap was available. Deficiencies in quality and quantity of water made well-digging necessary, and scarcity of proper tools made the task more laborious.[2]

DR. FUTCH *received his Ph.D. degree from Emory University in 1959, taught two years at Morehouse College, and is now on the history staff at the University of South Florida. His doctoral dissertation, from which this article was gleaned, was a study of Andersonville Prison, based largely on soldiers' letters and diaries.*

[1] For a description of the Andersonville stockade and of conditions prevailing there, see Ovid Futch, "Andersonville Raiders," *Civil War History*, II (1956), 47-48.

[2] Ransom A. Chadwick, "A Diary Kept in Andersonville Prison as a Member of the 85th New York Regiment," manuscript, Minnesota Historical Society Library, entries of June 27, July 2, 12, 1864 (hereafter cited as Chadwick, "Diary"); E. Merton Coulter (ed.), "From Spotsylvania Courthouse to Andersonville: A Diary of Darius Starr," *Georgia Historical Quarterly.* XLI (1957), 10 (hereafter cited as

Preparation of food consumed much time, owing to the shortage of cooking utensils. Lack of axes and saws made the procurement of wood for cooking and heating a toilsome task. The high mortality rate made necessary an occasional reorganization of the prison. This meant taking men from higher-numbered detachments to fill up the ranks of lower-numbered ones which had been depleted by the grim reaper. This "squadding over," as the prisoners called it, took all day and was much dreaded by the men because they had to remain in ranks until it was completed. But when they had done all that their captors required of them, and all they could do to satisfy their basic physical requirements, many waking hours remained to be filled, and prisoners complained, understandably, of time resting heavily on their hands.

If one may judge from their diaries, the things which interested Andersonville prisoners most were the prospects of exchange or parole, rations, the weather, and health. These were the subjects of many conversations while the men lolled about the stockade. New arrivals often busied themselves hatching plans for escape; in most cases, however, hope of eluding the guards soon waned. When the prison was first established the Confederates considered it insecure. Hoping to deter any outbreak, they told their captives that exchange was imminent. This was an old story to prisoners coming from Belle Isle; while they did not believe it, their hopes, nevertheless, remained alive.

When new prisoners arrived, inmates swarmed around them to hear the latest news of exchange or parole, as well as to learn about progress of the war and to look for relatives or acquaintances. But the Confederates labored diligently at strengthening the stockade. In early May, 1864, a prisoner who had arrived at Andersonville before the stockade was completed, and who had noted the continued efforts to increase its security, expressed doubt that getting out was any longer possible. He added wistfully: "Rebel officers now say that we are not going to be exchanged during the war, and as they can hold us now and no fear of escape, they had just as soon tell us the truth as not, and we must take things just as they see fit to give them to us."[3]

Still, newly-arrived prisoners were constantly bringing reports that buoyed the hopes of some. The smallest tidbit of news about exchange was repeated over and over, and was so liberally embellished that it soon became a general and imminent exchange. Although these rumors always proved false, some prisoners believed them helpful in sustaining life. A realistic outlook is reflected in the observation of one prisoner

"Starr Diary"); Eugene Forbes, *Diary of a Soldier and Prisoner of War in the Rebel Prisons* (Trenton, 1865), pp. 11, 17, 27. Hereafter cited as Forbes, *Diary of a Soldier.*

[3] John L. Ransom, *Andersonville Diary* . . . (Auburn, N.Y., 1881), pp. 41-42, 47, 54.

who wrote: "There is considerable excitement this mornng about Paroling, but it is all gass I reckon for there never was so ignorant a lot of men to gether since the World stood that is in reguard to matters outside of the Bull Pen." But this same prisoner did not hesitate to speculate on the state of affairs in the guards' camp. After noting the departure from Andersonville in mid-August of a number of Confederate troops bound for the front, he added: "The Rebs are trying to pull the wool over our eyes by sticking up Notices that there will be a Parole Imidately so as to keep the Boys from makeing a break dam their lying hearts this isn't the first time we have Guarded our selves since we came into the Bull Pen."[4]

Next to prospects of freedom, the most popular topic of conversation among Andersonville prisoners seems to have been food. They cursed the rations, discussed ways and means of preparing them so as to render them more palatable, and talked over prospects of an improvement in prison fare. Men boasted of the cooking prowess of their wives and mothers and made elaborately detailed plans of the sumptuous feasts they would enjoy on their return home. When food was issued uncooked, groups of prisoners pooled their rations and cooked them together to conserve firewood. Frequently they held animated discussions over the question of how to prepare the food. Some liked to make mush of the meal; some thought dumplings less distasteful; others preferred bread. On occasion they settled the matter by making all three and, in addition, scorching some of the meal and using it as coffee.[5]

When all had made their guesses concerning exchange and parole, the subject of rations had been exhausted, and nothing remained to be said about the weather, prisoners frequently turned to discussions of health. They bemoaned the filthy condition of the prison, their own deteriorating health, and the rising mortality rate. Many of them had their own theories about how to avoid sickness. Some thought it extremely important to remain cheerful and to avoid thoughts of home and past pleasures. One prisoner attributed his healthy condition to careful abstinence from tainted food and impure water. Some placed great faith in regular exercise, an occupation which crowded conditions made diffi-

---

[4] David Kennedy, "Diary of David Kennedy, Kept by Him While a Prisoner at Andersonville," manuscript Minnesota Historical Society Library, entry for May 11, 1864 (hereafter cited as Kennedy, "Diary"); Donald F. Danker (ed.), "Imprisoned at Andersonville: The Diary of Albert Harry Shatzel, May 5—September, 1864," *Nebraska History*, XXXVIII (1957), 115-16, 120 (hereafter cited as "Shatzel Diary"); J. M. Burdick, "Journal of Sgt. J. M. Burdick," manuscript in possession of Richard J. Harris, Swainsboro, Ga., entries for July 12, 18, Aug. 4, 1864. Hereafter cited as "Burdick Journal."

[5] For example, see Ransom, *Andersonville Diary*, p. 43; Job McElroy, *Andersonville: A Story of Rebel Military Prisons* (Toledo, 1879), . 342-44; Forbes, *Diary of a Soldier*, pp. 18, 22.

cult. A few relied heavily on keeping as clean as possible, others took cathartics, and one confessed: "Why I am sustained is a mystery to me."[6]

Topics of great interest were the latest reports from the field of battle. New prisoners, who occasionally brought copies of old newspapers with them, arrived to find themselves swamped with inquiries concerning military activities. Confederate guards sometimes gave or sold papers to prisoners. These papers had wide circulation; the stockade inmates excitedly discussed their contents, scoffing at the prejudiced presentation of news in Southern journals. Prisoners frequently heard war news from guards, but they placed little reliance on information from that source. Optimistic rumors of war developments were as wild and unreliable as those concerning exchange. As early as May, 1864, reports circulated in the stockade that Atlanta and Richmond had fallen.[7]

Other subjects were not lacking to engage those inclined to conversation. Some prisoners were so fond of relating past experiences that their life histories became well known to bored acquaintances. Sailors told tall stories of the sea; foreigners and others who had traveled in distant lands described alien places and peoples and customs. Some demonstrated their vituperative talents in denouncing the South in general, and the keepers of Andersonville Prison in particular. Still others seemed unable to converse without speaking longingly of loved ones at home. Another topic which absorbed the attention of many prisoners was the possibility of escape.

Three hundred and twenty-nine prisoners escaped from Andersonville Prison during its existence. A far greater number got away temporarily, but permanent escape was rendered exceedingly difficult by the remoteness of Andersonville from Union lines and the efficiency of the dogs which Confederates used to track runaways.[8] Most of the prisoners who escaped did so by running off from outside work details, or by violating their paroles not to escape while employed outside the stockade. Some got away by bribing guards, others simply by walking off after returning tools from the stockade at the end of the day. But for the vast majority of prisoners, the only hope of escape seemed to be through tunneling. To this activity they devoted much time and effort.

---

[6] Chadwick, "Diary," entries for May 17-Sept. 5, 1864, passim; Kennedy, "Diary," entries for May 4-Sept. 6, 1864, passim; Burdick, "Journal," entries for July 31, Aug. 20, 31, Sept. 2, 1864; McElroy, Andersonville, pp. 154-55. See also C. M. Destler (ed.), "A Vermonter in Andersonville: Diary of Charles Ross, 1864," Vermont History, XXV (1957), 239. Hereafter cited as "Ross Diary."

[7] For example, see Chadwick, "Diary," entries for May 27, June 22, July 10, Sept. 2, 1864; "Shatzel Diary," p. 93.

[8] "Andersonville, Ga. Rolls of Deceased Federal Prisoners, 1864-65," Box 20, Record Group 249, National Archives; Columbus (Ga.) Daily Enquirer, May 12, 1864. See also U.S. War Dept. (comp.), War of the Rebellion: A Compilation of the Official Records of the Union and Confederate Armies (Washington, 1880-1901), Ser. II, VII, 438, 517, 708. Hereafter cited as OR, with all references being to Ser. II.

When a group of prisoners decided to engage in a "tunnel operation," they tried to get a spot near the deadline from which to begin. If they had quarters large enough to permit, they might start digging under their shelter. If not, they pretended to be in search of water, and after digging a "well," struck out horizontally from its side. Seriously handicapped by lack of tools, they were forced to use such implements as sharp sticks, knives, and canteen halves. A group of tunnelers who obtained an old fire shovel considered themselves very fortunate. Only one man at a time could dig in the narrow burrow; as a result progress was very slow. As the tunnel lengthened, men lined up behind the digger to pass back the loosened earth which was surreptitiously dumped into the creek flowing through the stockade. When the tunnel's owners considered it long enough to open, they chose their night to go through. After their passage any other prisoners who desired to do so might use the tunnel, for the more men getting out, the greater the chance of confusing the dogs and enabling the first ones through the tunnel to make good their escape.[9]

Tunneling was a hazardous venture. Digging was difficult to conceal and detection led to serious punishment. Moreover, the soil was subject to cave-ins. If one got out through a tunnel, he ran the risk of being shot or, if recaptured, having to wear a ball and chain or being put in the stocks or chain gang. On one occasion some prisoners had completed a long tunnel and were preparing to break out when a cave-in trapped the sergeant who had gone to open the tunnel. According to a member of the sergeant's mess, "he had to dig out & when he came out the Reb guard took him down to Hd Qr's & now he is in the stocks hard but honest." Four days later this philosophical diarist recorded the opening of another tunnel and added: "100 of the Boys left last night & 2 more were going out this morning & they were shot. poor Boys such is life. some die one way & some another."[10]

After the recapture and return of several men who had been out about twelve days, one prisoner noted that "they all have balls and chains; there must be now nearly 100 men wearing these articles." But at least one of those condemned to wear the ball and chain for attempting to escape was able to deceive the Confederates. As soon as they returned him to the stockade and departed, he lost himself in the crowd and removed the ball and chain. Thenceforth he wore the shackles only when reporting to the gate each morning at nine o'clock for inspection.[11]

John Ransom, a sergeant in the 9th Michigan Cavalry, after involv-

[9] Ransom, *Andersonville Diary*, p. 47; Forbes, *Diary of a Soldier*, pp. 12-13; McElroy, *Andersonville*, pp. 175-78; Robert H. Kellogg, *Life and Death in Rebel Prisons* (Hartford, 1865), pp. 118-21.

[10] "Shatzel Diary," pp. 112-13.

[11] Forbes, *Diary of a Soldier*, p. 16; Ransom, *Andersonville Diary*, p. 69.

ment in a tunneling project which was abandoned because "the location was not practicable," joined another group of tunnelers. The second
venture was successful and the cavalryman went out with a friend one
dark night shortly before daylight. When the two had crawled some 200
or 250 yards from the stockade, they were startled by the guards firing at
others prisoners coming out of the tunnel. They jumped up and ran,
"seemingly making more noise than a troop of cavalry." When the first
light appeared in the east, they had traveled only about three miles,
were covered with mud and scratches, and could hear the yelping dogs
on their trail. Ransom afterward wrote: "In a few moments the hounds
came up with us and began smelling of us. [They] did not offer to bite
us." Soon five mounted Confederates arrived and escorted the forlorn
prisoners back to the prison to see the Confederate captain in charge of
the stockade. "After cussing us a few minutes," wrote Ransom, "we were
put in the chain gang, where we remained two days." Although the
chain gang was not exactly pleasant, he found it "not so bad after all.
We had more to eat than when inside, and we had shade to lay in, and
although my ankles were made very sore, do not regret my escapade."[12]

The prison keepers frequently sent Negroes into the stockade to check
the wells and search for tunnels which, when found, had to be dug out
and filled in. Either the Negroes were not greatly interested in discover-
ing tunnels or the prisoners were remarkably clever in concealing them.
On July 20 a prisoner wrote: "A tunnel was opened this A. M., about two
o'clock, and men were escaping until after daylight, when the guard discovered them and gave the alarm." Though Negroes probed wells and
looked for more tunnels that day, a group of prisoners opened another
one after dark. But no one escaped on this occasion. In their eagerness
to get out, about 500 men congregated near the tunnel entrance, arous-
ing the suspicions of the guards and defeating their own purpose. Some
of the guards were deficient in vigilance and a few of them helped prisoners to escape. The stockade inmates noted one night that seven sentry
posts were silent. The next day a prisoner recorded in his diary: "This
morning it was ascertained that fourteen of our men had 'tunneled out,'
and that seven guards had accompanied them, taking their arms and ac-
coutrements."[13]

On the other hand, some tunnel projects were thwarted by traitors, or
"turncoats," among the prisoners themselves. Psychological and medical
studies of the effects of confinement and dietary deficiencies on the behavior of prisoners in World War II and the Korean conflict help to explain disloyalty at Andersonville. These studies show that human life
requires the maintenance of a satisfactory body temperature, adequate
intake of food, fluids, and air, satisfactory elimination of wastes, a satis-

[12] Ibid., pp. 50, 52.   [13] Forbes, Diary of a Soldier, pp. 20, 22, 32.

factory amount of rest and activity, and satisfactory relationships with other human beings. Failure to meet these conditions results in various physical discomforts and in fear, anxiety, anger, loneliness, sadness, and dejection. Men placed in a situation like Andersonville Prison, which upsets these relationships and produces extreme pressures, sometimes follow a pattern of reaction, the final stage of which is exasperation, dejection, and unreasoning dependence upon any offer of help. In this condition, which psychologists call "situation of frustration," a man is "emotionally bankrupt," at the "end of his rope," and unusually receptive to approval or human support. He will do anything to win approval of those human beings in whose power he finds himself. Deprivation of food contributes directly to this "situation of frustration."[14] Considering the conditions that existed in the Andersonville stockade, it is not surprising that some prisoners turned informers.

"Tunnel-traitors" were useful to the Confederates and a thorn in the side of fellow prisoners. It was not unusual for a tunnel to be reported just when its diggers were ready to reap the fruit of their labors. On one occasion, in mid-June, 1864, some thirty prisoners were preparing to open their tunnel when one of their number betrayed them. Shortly afterwards one of the disappointed conspirators wrote in his diary that "the devil is to pay again for the Rebel Serg't found the Tunnel where a 200 of us was going out to Night. god help the man that informs on this party. if he is found he is going up the first pot sure."[15]

Nor was this an idle threat. Informers, when caught, received rough treatment at the hands of fellow prisoners. A New York cavalry sergeant wrote in mid-July: "Today a tunnel was discovered by the rebel authorities, 4 of the prisoners had dug a well 60 feet deep, about 20 feet down they had struck out dug 20 feet outside the stockade and were a going to escape in 10 nights, one of our men betrayed them for a plug of tobacco." A new Jersey infantry sergeant recorded the same incident, adding that other prisoners shaved the hair off half of the traitor's head, branded the letter "T" on his forehead, and marched him about the camp for all to see.[16] A Michigan cavalry sergeant wrote of an informer whose punishment was more serious:

A lame man, for telling of a tunnel, was pounded almost to death last night, and this morning they were chasing him to administer more punishment, when he ran inside the dead line claiming protection of the guard. The

---

[14] Lawrence E. Hinkle, Jr., and Harold G. Wolff, "Communist Interrogation and Indoctrination of 'Enemies of the State,'" *A.M.A. Archives of Neurology and Psychiatry*, LXXVI (1956), 130, 170-71; Bruno Bettelheim, "Individual and Mass Behavior in Extreme Situations," *Journal of Abnormal and Social Psychology*, XXXVIII (1943), 438-39, 447.

[15] "Shatzel Diary," pp. 101, 103.

[16] Burdick, "Journal," entry for July 16, 1864; Forbes, *Diary of a Soldier*, p. 31.

guard didn't protect worth a cent, but shot him through the head. A general hurrahing took place, as the rebel had only saved our men the trouble of killing him.[17]

The number of traitors in the stockade was large enough to render impracticable any organized plan of escape involving a large number of prisoners. In late May, 1864, a plot was devised to execute a grand break by undermining the stockade so that at a given signal the conspirators could rush forward and push over several palisades, capture the batteries, overpower the guard, and release other prisoners. It was a daring plan, possibly a foolhardy one. Yet at that time the Confederate regulars had recently left Andersonville for Richmond and the prison was guarded by undisciplined reserves whom many prisoners expected to abandon their posts and take to the woods at the first sign of a determined uprising. But the break was not made. A traitor disclosed the plot to prison authorities, who had the tunnels destroyed. To discourage any further outbreak, Captain Henry Wirz, the prison commander, had the following notice posted inside the stockade:

Not wishing to shed the blood of hundreds not connected with those who concocted a plan to force the stockade, and make in this way their escape, I hereby warn the leaders and those who formed themselves into a band to carry out this, that I am in possession of all the facts, and have made arrangements accordingly, so to frustrate it. No choice would be left me but to open with grape and canister on the stockade, and what effect this would have in this densely crowded place need not be told.[18]

In mid-July Captain Wirz summoned the mess sergeants to his headquarters and informed them that, although his government was eager to exchange prisoners, the United States would not do so because the enlistment terms of many Federal prisoners had expired. Assuring them that he had enough rations to feed them for two years if necessary, Wirz warned the prisoners that an attempted break would be suicide. In the words of Sergeant Eugene Forbes, he "stated that . . . if the attempt were made, he would open on the stockade with grape and canister so long as a man were left alive within it." Such threats made many prisoners apprehensive. About two o'clock that afternoon, Confederate artillerymen fired two cannons as a signal for guards to man their stations and demonstrate how well prepared they were to repel an uprising.

[17] Ransom, *Andersonville Diary*, pp. 56-57. See also K. C. Bullard, *Over the Dead-Line, Or Who Killed "Poll Parrot"* (New York, 1909), pp. 16-17, 31-32. Eighteen feet inside the stockade wall, the "deadline" was a row of posts set in the earth and connected by boards across their tops. Almost every prison, North and South, had its deadline.

[18] Chadwick, "Diary," entry for May 25, 1864; Kennedy, "Diary," entry for May 27, 1864; Ransom, *Andersonville Diary*, pp. 65-66; McElroy, *Andersonville*, pp. 193-94; Kellogg, *Life and Death in Rebel Prisons*, pp. 105-06.

Federal prisoners at Andersonville, Georgia. These drawings, from the 1913 edition of John McElroy's *Andersonville*, were presumably made from contemporary photographs. Bottom view shows some of the prisoners' shelters partly supported by the rail designating the "dead line."

Rock Island Prison Barracks, Illinois, from a lithograph of 1864. This view faces west, or downriver, with the city of Rock Island in the background and the Iowa side to the right. The actual stockade surrounds the square of barracks labeled "1."

Roll call at Rock Island Prison. The garrison roll call squad stands in foreground, with Confederate prisoners mustered beside their quarters in rear. At left is the ditch designating the "dead line," which lay inside the west wall of the stockade just out of the picture to the left.

Confederate prisoners at Fort Warren, Boston Harbor, in 1863 or 1864. The men identified by numbers are (bottom row) "1." Cornelius Galloway Smith of Georgia, captured blockade runner, "2." George W. Davis, another blockade runner, and (top row) "3." Edward John Johnston, an Irishman who died and was buried in the fort. From *Confederate Veteran* (1908).

Libby Prison, Richmond, Virginia, from a sketch by a returned Federal prisoner. The tents in foreground are for the guards. From *Harper's Weekly* (1863).

Prison camp at Elmira, New York. This is the view from an observation platform built on a public road outside the camp, from which curious civilians gained glimpses of the Confederates for 10¢ per peek. From *Harper's Weekly* (1865).

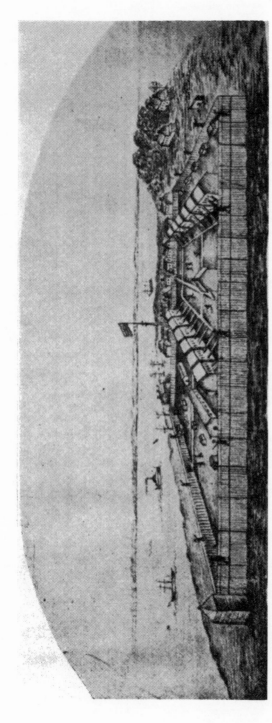

Johnson's Island prison, in Lake Erie off Sandusky, Ohio. A sketch by a Confederate prisoner. From *Confederate Veteran* (1896).

The yard of the city jail, Charleston, South Carolina, where Federal Lt. Edmund E. Ryan was confined in September, 1864. A contemporary print.

Many prisoners thought it was the beginning of a massacre. Forbes afterward wrote:

Sergeants engaged in issuing rations, dropped their cups or knives, and fell flat to the ground, rooting their noses into mother earth like babies for their "titty," men plunged headlong into the "dug out" tents, the brook, or any place that offered the least show, or, in fact, no show for shelter against the storm of grape and canister which they expected was soon to come hurtling over their devoted heads; cries of "lie down" and other vociferations resounded through all parts of the camp, and the writer hereof felt very much as if he would as soon be somewhere else, to say the very least.[19]

An Illinois cavalryman wrote fifteen years later that the cannon firing "was answered with a yell of defiance from ten thousand throats," and that the prisoners stood "erect, excited, defiant." Perhaps a fairly accurate idea of their reaction may be gotten from the diary of a prisoner:

The Rebbs tried to show us how smart they Could be shot 12 lb guns (as a signal; it took them ¼ hour to fall in) we could take all they have got here in half that time they scared some of our boys half to Death while others called the rebbs every thing they Could and laughed at them and they soon played out.[20]

Apparently some of the guards, as well as residents of the neighborhood, were not informed of the drill. According to one prisoner, "as soon as the alarm was given, they commenced 'skedaddling' for the woods, making as good time as a quarter horse."

After some thirty minutes of tumult, "everything relapsed into the usual state of semi-confusion." The drill, insofar as it was intended to impress the prisoners, was not very successful. One private observed that "the Johneys . . . fired their Artillery & raised the devil generaly for a spell then returned to their Qr's & all they can muster hear is about 2500."[21]

Prisoners had a very low opinion of the Georgia Reserves who guarded them. Relations of captives with captors which, prior to replacement of Confederate regulars at Andersonville by reserves, had been as pleasant as could be expected under the circumstances, deteriorated rapidly when the undisciplined recruits took over. One prisoner, after describing the suffering he endured en route to Andersonville, wrote: "we are under the Malishia & their ages range from 10 to 75 years & they are the Dambdst set of men I ever have had the Luck to fall in with yet . . . God help the Prisoner when they fall into the hands of the Malishia." Another wrote that "perched upon the stockade as guards"

[19] Forbes, *Diary of a Soldier*, p. 30.
[20] McElroy, *Andersonville*, p. 196; Chadwick, "Diary," entry for July 14, 1864.
[21] Forbes, *Diary of a Soldier*, p. 30; "Shatzel Diary," p. 112.

were "the worst looking scallawags . . . , from boys just large enough to handle a gun, to old men who ought to have been dead years ago for the good of their country." A third characterized his guards as "the off scourings of the South," and added: "They act as though they were scared to death at the sight of a Yankee." According to a fourth, some sentries on duty in late July were barely able to see over the stockade, "being 14 or 15 years old and very small."[22]

Prisoners were especially critical of the alacrity with which the reserves fired on men crossing or reaching over the "deadline." So trigger-happy were some of the sentinels that their captives believed the false rumor that guards received a thirty-day furlough for each Yankee they killed. Of course the prisoners were prejudiced in their judgments, but the testimony of Confederate observers substantiates both the unsoldierly qualities of the reserve troops and their excessive zeal for shooting. Captain Wirz complained of their "carelessness" and "inefficiency" and asserted that their "worthlessness" was "on the increase day by day." General John H. Winder, commanding officer of the prison post, bemoaned their lack of discipline and reported to Richmond that he could not depend on them.[23] Charles H. Thiot, a Chatham County, Georgia planter, serving as an enlisted man in the 1st Georgia Regiment, wrote his wife that some reserves had "no more sense than to shoot [prisoners] if they dare cross the line just to pick up a ball or empty a washpan." Two days later Thiot added that "some of them would like nothing better than to shoot one of the scoundrels just for the fun of it. Indeed, I heard one chap say that he just wanted one to put his foot over the line when he was on post, and he would never give him time to pull it back. Many would murder them in cold blood."[24]

One member of the reserves, Private James E. Anderson, was so distressed by the frequent shootings at the deadline that he wrote the following complaint to President Jefferson Davis:

We have many thoughtless boys here who think the killing of a Yankee will make them great men. . . . Every day or two there are prisoners shot. When the officer of the guard goes to the sentry stand, there is a dead or badly wounded man invariably within their own lines. The sentry, of course, says he was across the dead-line when he shot him. . . . Last Sabbath there were two shot in their tents at one shot. The boy said that he shot at one across the deadline. Night before last there was one shot near me (I being on guard). The sentry said that the Yankee made one step across the line to avoid a mud hole. He shot him through the bowels, and when the officer

[22] Ibid., pp. 91-92; Ransom, Andersonville Diary, p. 47; Kennedy, "Diary," entry for May 25, 1864; Forbes, Diary of a Soldier, p. 34.
[23] OR, VII, 410, 451, 708.
[24] Thiot to his wife, May 7, 9, 1864, manuscript in possession of Charles T. Winship, Atlanta, Ga.

of the guard got there he was lying inside their own lines. He [the sentry] as usual told him that he stepped across, but fell back inside.[25]

The Sunday shooting of two men in a tent, to which Anderson referred, occurred on June 19, 1864. Eugene Forbes, an inmate who recorded the incident in his diary, averred that a prisoner obtained permission of the sentry to cross the deadline for the purpose of killing a snake and that another guard fired from a distant post, missed the snake killer, and injured two men in a tent, one in the head, the other in the thigh.

Private Harry Shatzel wrote on June 22: "there was 3 men shot dead last night & there wasn't one of them inside of the dead line." On another occasion Eugene Forbes reported a guard firing at a prisoner who pushed a piece of wood over the deadline and added that the "rebel sergeant told the sentry he was a fool and never did know his business." One sentinel accidentally fired his gun and hit a prisoner who was in the act of taking his pipe from his mouth. The ball cut his thumb, finger, cheek, and tongue. Another shot himself by accident. Firing by sentinels was very common indeed, especially at night, but many of the shots did no physical damage.[26]

Occasionally citizens of the region, both male and female, came to visit the prison and to get a look at the "Yanks." One prisoner observed "sympathy in some of their faces and in some a lack of it." Among these visitors were members of the Americus Ladies Aid Society, who went to Andersonville to carry food to sick Confederate soldiers. While there they visited the cemetery to watch the burial of dead Federals and climbed the sentry box ladders to gaze down upon the unfortunate prisoners. These ladies grieved over the sick and dying soldiers of the Confederacy, but the sympathy of some did not extend to the stockade inmates. One young beauty who went up to see the Yankees was Miss Hallie Clayton of Americus. A woman who accompanied her wrote years later that Miss Clayton "was disposed to say ugly things to them & glory at their being captured, and imprisoned." Visitors declined in number with the passing of time, as few were willing to endure the stench which eventually enshrouded the filthy stockade.[27]

Prison life would have been less dreary for many if reading material had been plentiful, but those who wished to read had little or no choice.

[25] *OR*, VII, 403.

[26] Forbes, *Diary of a Soldier*, pp. 12, 18, 21-29, 30-36, 40-45; "Shatzel Diary," pp. 94, 100, 104-05, 115; Kennedy, "Diary," entries for June 22, July 4, 18, 27, Aug. 2, 1864; Chadwick, "Diary," entries for May 2, July 13, 1864; Ransom, *Andersonville Diary*, p. 86. See also *The Trial of Henry Wirz*, 40th Cong., 2nd Sess., House Executive Document 23 (Washington, 1868), p. 497. Hereafter cited as *Wirz Trial*.

[27] Ransom, *Andersonville Diary*, pp. 44, 78; "Reminiscence of Mrs. Florence Hollis," manuscript in possession of Robert C. Pendergrass, Americus, Ga.

Bibles and New Testaments seem to have outnumbered all other books combined within the stockade, and many inmates found a measure of solace in perusing the Scriptures. Charles Ross, of Lower Waterford, Vermont, wrote in his diary one Saturday: "Have read a good lot in the Bible today. Am not through with the book of Isiah. I am getting more proffit from such reading than a little." Another Vermonter wrote on August 30 that he had "finished reading the Testament for the first time in my Natchrel life," and on the next day, had started it again. Perhaps the most sought-after reading materials were newspapers, especially from the North, but they were few and far between. Illinois Cavalryman John McElroy wrote years later that the only thing he could get to read was a copy of *Gray's Anatomy*. Other prisoners managed to obtain a *History of America*, Milton's *Paradise Lost*, and Bunyan's *Pilgrim's Progress*.[28]

Mail, the reading matter which would have afforded the greatest pleasure, was exceedingly scarce. Prisoners were permitted to write one-page letters. They received both correspondence and packages, but deliveries were very infrequent and all mail was carefully censored. Outgoing letters informed the recipient of the prisoner's whereabouts and gave assurances of his well-being. Some writers gave the place and date of their capture or the names of other Andersonville prisoners known to the addressee. One stated that writing news was not permitted and that if it were he had none to write. Another instructed his parents: "Write ... nothing but family matters and no longer than I have written. leave the envelope open so to be Inspected by the Confederate authorities." A foreign-born member of a New York regiment wrote his brother: "tha donet low us to Rite Only So much Right as Son as you Can and in Ingles Becos tha Rede Ol the latars Befor we git tham."[29]

A Michigan cavalry sergeant who had reasonably good penmanship was importuned by his fellow inmates to write letters to Wirz, General Winder, President Davis, and other Confederate officials describing the woeful circumstances of individual prisoners and begging for release. A Pennsylvania cavalryman paroled as hospital steward managed, "through the kindness of a friend," to send an uncensored letter. He wrote: "Don't be uneasy about me. I am going to live it through—about

[28] Ransom, *Andersonville Diary*, pp. 46, 50, 68; "Ross Diary," pp. 236, 240; "Shatzel Diary," pp. 122-23; John W. Northrop, "Diary of Prison Life at Andersonville during the Civil War," manuscript, Western Reserve Historical Society, entry for May 25, 1864.

[29] Record Group 109, National Archives, Ch. IX, V, 227, pp. 1, 13, 30, 33, 35; Spencer B. King, Jr. (ed.), "Yankee Letters from Andersonville Prison," *Georgia Historical Quarterly*, XXXVIII (1954), 395-98; Louis Manigault Scrapbook, 1861-65, South Caroliniana Library, pp. 219-24; W. R. Worth to Mrs. William Worth, July 8, 1864, Louis A. Bringier Papers, Louisiana State University.

12,000 of our brave boys died in this place this summer. . . . You can judge how they must be situated and treated. I will some day be able to tell you all about it." Another Pennsylvanian, S. J. Gibson, whose letter was passed by the censor, contrived to make it clear that Andersonville was difficult to endure. He wrote his wife: "it is my misfortune still to be held a Prisoner of War; Our condition is by no means a desirable one; . . . We try to be as cheerful and contented as we can, . . . Give yourself no uneasiness concerning *me*; I can live where any other man can."[30]

Correspondence consumed relatively little of the Andersonville prisoners' time, and in the struggle with ennui they turned to various other activities. To avoid having to draw rations in caps or shoes, those who could get old pieces of stovepipe or tin twisted them into dishes. Many carved wooden spoons. One prisoner later wrote that he and a friend carved chess pieces out of roots from the swamp along the creek, blackened one set with soot, obtained a wide plank which was usable as a board, and found in playing chess a way of temporarily forgetting some of the misery surrounding them. Some spent much time visiting and ministering to sick prisoners. Others took frequent walks, looking for old acquaintances or merely observing life in the stockade. A prison diarist reported seeing small gardens of beans and corn, no more than three inches wide, planted around three sides of some tents. A Michigan printer enjoyed spreading his ration of cow peas out on a blanket and picking them up one by one as fast as he could, as if picking up type. One hindrance to this pastime was his habit of unconsciously putting the peas in his mouth. "In this way," he wrote, "I often eat up the whole printing office." He found another printer in prison and the two sometimes had "pea-picking" contests. Some prisoners occupied themselves by carving ornaments from bone or wood with knives made from iron hoops. Others drew sketches with rude pens dipped in ink made from rust.[31]

Despite the absence of any chaplain in the stockade, some of the prisoners held religious services on their own. In May, 1864, Reverend William John Hamilton, a Catholic priest who lived in Macon and whose mission included all of southwestern Georgia, visited Andersonville. Finding a large number of Catholic prisoners there, he asked the Bishop of Savannah to send priests to minister to them. He returned the following week and spent three days giving to Catholic inmates the consolations of their religion. In June, Bishop Augustin Verot of Savannah sent

[30] Ransom, *Andersonville Diary*, p. 69; James T. Harnit to Albert R. Kelly, Nov. 15, 1864, Ohio Historical Society; S. J. Gibson to Mrs. Rachel A. Gibson, June 12, 1864, Library of Congress.

[31] McElroy, *Andersonville*, pp. 213-14; Chadwick, "Diary," entry for June 2, 1864; Forbes, *Diary of a Soldier*, pp. 15, 17, 23; New York *Times*, Sept. 5, 1864.

another priest, Reverend Peter Whelan, to minister to Catholic prisoners. Finding himself unable to attend to their spiritual needs, Father
Whelan wrote to Savannah for help, and the bishop sent a Father Claveril to assist him.

The priests won the sincere admiration of most prisoners, of whatever
faith. One inmate observed that smallpox cases received the same attention as any others. "The priests are in every day," another wrote, "and
are the only Christian professors who visit the camp." The Holy Fathers
frequently had to get down on hands and knees and crawl into dug-outs
in order to hear confessions. Sometimes they had to administer extreme
unction while lying alongside sick or dying prisoners. Some non-Catholic
residents of the countryside were ashamed because none of their clergy
visited the prison. When once asked why ministers of other denomina-
tions did not make prison rounds, Bishop Verot, who twice visited the
stockade himself, wrote that "error, sterile by its nature, will not pro-
duce the rush of charity proportionate to the extent of the needs."

Father Claveril soon fell ill and retired to Father Hamilton's residence
in Macon to recover. From Augusta came Father John Kirby to replace
him, but Kirby stayed only about two weeks. According to Father
Hamilton, one "could find every nationality inside the stockade," and the
clergymen were disturbed by their inability to communicate with prisoners who could not understand English. After Father Kirby's departure, a
Jesuit from Spring Hill College near Mobile, Alabama, Father Hosannah,
who could speak a number of languages, came to Andersonville. He and
Father Whelan remained until near the end of September, 1864, when
most of the prisoners had been removed. As a result of the labors of these
devoted men, the Savannah bishop was able to proclaim that "many
Protestants and many unbelievers had the good fortune of conversion to
our holy religion and received baptism."[32]

A Methodist missionary to Florida troops in the Confederate army,
Reverend E. B. Duncan, addressed the Andersonville prisoners on two
occasions. Visiting the post in early August for the purpose of expound-
ing the gospel to the company of Florida artillery stationed there,
Duncan delivered a sermon in the stockade from atop a box near the
sutler's stand. Again in January, 1865, when only about 5,000 captives
remained at Andersonville, he stopped on his way to Florida and spent
three evenings conducting religious services for the Confederate troops.
Before leaving he preached to the stockade inmates and, briefly, to the
patients in the prison hospital. Of his second adventure in the stockade,
Duncan wrote to a fellow minister:

[32] Ransom, *Andersonville Diary*, p. 47; Eliza Francis Andrews, *The War-Time
Journal of a Georgia Girl* (New York, 1908), pp. 77-78; *Wirz Trial*, pp. 290, 293,
426, 430; *Annales de la Propagation de la Foi*, XXXVII (1865), 398-99.

They stood up round me, while I stood on a box and declared to them the Gospel . . . I had unusual liberty, and they listened with most profound attention. At the close I invited them to seek religion and come to God, when the ground was literally covered with them that prostrated themselves. But few in that vast assembly remained standing. . . . They treated me with the greatest respect, thanking me kindly and begging me to return, and followed me when leaving as if loath to let me go. Many came to shake hands, until, like the Indian, I said, "I shake hands in my heart."[33]

During the spring of 1864, a few prisoners started holding prayer meetings and attempting to preach; by mid-July these meetings had attracted a large following. It became more or less customary to hold prayer meetings and preaching services on alternate nights. These gatherings had no fixed location. At dusk the song leaders would go to the spot decided upon for that particular night and start some familiar hymn, whereupon interested prisoners would assemble. T. J. Shepherd, an Ohio prisoner who did a good deal of the preaching, later estimated that possibly 100 men were converted as a result of meetings with which he was connected. Also active in the services was Boston Corbett, later famous as the slayer of John Wilkes Booth. Prominent song leaders were Sergeant B. N. Waddell of Kenton, Ohio; David Atherton of New York; and J. C. Turner of Townline, Lucerne County, Pennsylvania.

In addition to prayer meetings and preaching services, pious prisoners also conducted funeral ceremonies, formed an organization to care for the sick, and met on Sunday mornings to study the Bible in an "Andersonville Sunday School." When a heavy August rain opened a fresh spring of water just inside the west deadline a short distance north of the creek, many prisoners considered it the result of divine intervention in answer to their prayers, and called the fount "Providence Spring."[34] Present day visitors to Andersonville Prison Park may still drink of its cool, free-flowing water.

[33] J. William Jones, *Christ in the Camp, or Religion in the Confederate Army* (Atlanta, 1904), p. 624; *Wirz Trial,* pp. 609-10; Forbes, *Diary of a Soldier,* p. 35; Chadwick, "Diary," entry for Aug. 1, 1864.

[34] John A. Mendenhall, "Diary of J. A. Mendenhall," Indiana Historical Society, entry for Aug. 20, 1864; McElroy, *Andersonville,* pp. 629-36; John W. Urban, *In Defense of the Union* (Chicago, 1887), p. 210.

THE MILITARY PRISON
AT FORT WARREN

Minor H. McLain

A prisoner-of-war station is unique in that within its confines soldiers of belligerent armies must live together as noncombatants while subject to constant and sometimes potentially explosive tensions. Under such circumstances a prisoner may come to hate his enemy with a fervor seldom equalled by soldiers on the battlefield. On the other hand, relations between guard and captive may attain a level of mutual respect that makes it possible for each to appreciate the other as a human being in spite of an irreconcilable division of loyalties. This seems to have been the prevailing pattern at Fort Warren, on George's Island in Boston Harbor, during the Civil War.

Originally this fort was constructed as part of the maritime defenses of Massachusetts. Built of granite in the pentagon shape common to early nineteenth century fortresses, its exterior impressed both Confederate prisoners and New England visitors with its strength. Nevertheless, many private citizens and public officials of Massachusetts often expressed anxiety during the war years about the fort's readiness to repel an enemy assault. Federal officials, aware of this concern, were nevertheless committed to a policy of giving greater priority to the more immediate requirements for the active prosecution of the war against the Confederate armed forces.[1]

In appraising any military prison, it is proper to compare the living conditions of the soldiers garrisoned there with those of the prisoners. A noticeable difference or similarity between the two may be an indication of the character of the detaining power or the commanding officer of the post. At the beginning of the Civil War, before its designation as a prison, Fort Warren was a training base for a number of Massachusetts regiments. Inadequate housing and food for large groups of incoming

---

DR. MINOR McLAIN's *interest in Civil War prisons stemmed in part from his own experiences as a prisoner of war in Germany during World War II. He is currently associate professor of history at the State College at Salem, Massachusetts. This article is a condensation of his doctoral thesis at Boston University.*

[1] Minor Horne McLain, "Prison Conditions in Fort Warren, Boston, during the Civil War" (Unpublished dissertation, Boston University, 1955), pp. 1-26.

men often resulted in complaints that were later echoed by newly arrived prisoners. A soldier of the 14th Massachusetts Infantry (which later became the 1st Massachusetts Heavy Artillery) wrote: "Our first night at the fort was one long to be remembered, no provision had been made for us and, as we had neither blankets nor overcoats, we were obliged to take the cold stone floor for bed with nothing to cover us, the cold wind blowing through the embrasures from the ocean."

The men of another company were issued blankets, but no bunks were ready for them. Unless they had friends in another unit with whom they might sleep, they also were obliged to sleep on the stone floor.[2] These accounts cannot be dismissed merely as customary soldier grumbling. The noted Dr. Samuel G. Howe inspected the quarters at about this time and reported to Governor John A. Andrew that while each soldier should "be allowed in his barrack 600 cubic feet of air," the figure at Fort Warren was "less than 145 feet." The physician thought some of the overcrowding was doubtless due to the speed with which newly recruited men were rushed there, and he commented further: "I omit from the calculation one room in which on one night seventy-five men are said to have slept with a floor space of only nine feet to a man; which is hardly credible even by western travellers who have to sleep three in a bed or on the floor."[3] Later, when Massachusetts assigned several artillery regiments to the fortress to defend that position and guard the prisoners, the enlisted men were relieved to find conditions more settled. Their quarters were better than anticipated; several rooms had bunks similar to those on fishing vessels, with mattresses made of sacks and filled with straw.

Army rations are seldom praised, and those issued at Fort Warren were no exception. The men received the regulation fresh beef with potatoes three times a week, salt beef, pork or ham three times weekly, and baked beans on Sunday. Each man was entitled to tea and coffee as well as twenty-two ounces of bread per day, but there were instances of the weekly rations lasting for only six days—which led to quarreling between the cooks and soldiers of the battalion. Following investigation of one complaint later in the war, an aide to the governor issued a statement that it was simply a matter of the usual difference between army and civilian food.[4]

The Lincoln administration's efforts to check subversion behind the lines directly affected Fort Warren's role as a war prison—as did also

[2] A. S. Roe and Charles Nutt, *History of the First Regiment of Heavy Artillery* (Worcester, 1917), p. 8.
[3] S. G. Howe, *A Letter of the Sanitary Condition of the Troops in the Neighborhood of Boston . . .* (Washington, 1861), p. 8.
[4] *Cape Ann Advertiser*, Dec. 24 and 27, 1861; Governor of Massachusetts, *Letters Official*, LI (1864), 478. Hereafter cited as *Letters Official*.

the shift of military fortune in favor of the Union. Shortly after the conflict began, the fear of disloyalty in the North led to many political arrests, especially in the border state of Maryland. Meanwhile, the Union army captured the Confederate fort at Hatteras Island, North Carolina. Massachusetts received its first intimation of the impending arrival of prisoners from both these actions when Governor Andrew was officially requested to send a contingent to Fort Warren for guard duty. Colonel Justin E. Dimick, a professional soldier who up to this time had been commanding officer at Fortress Monroe, was transferred to the command of the Massachusetts fort. The orders forwarded to him on October 19, 1861, contained seven points on procedure: 1) the prisoners were to be "securely held," but were to be "treated with all kindness"; 2) adequate records should be kept in connection with all of them; 3) prisoners would be allowed to provide themselves with such comforts as they required and could afford, and they might receive, subject to inspection, articles of food, clothing and small sums of money not exceeding twenty dollars at a time; 4) they might have newspapers and send and receive letters subject to certain censorship provisions; 5) visitors were permitted upon receipt of authorization from Washington and with an officer present; 6) released prisoners must be examined to prevent the transmission of secret messages; and 7) detailed records of food and clothing issued each prisoner must be kept. The instructions also required Colonel Dimick to resist all efforts to release either military or political prisoners by a writ of habeas corpus. Coincidentally with the transmission of these orders, Captain George A. Kensel, the United States Quartermaster in Boston, was instructed to prepare rations for 100 prisoners for a thirty-day period.[5]

On October 27, 1861, prisoners of war at Fort Columbus in New York harbor learned that they were to be transferred to Fort Warren. Three days later they were taken on board the State of Maine, which had already picked up the political prisoners from Fort Lafayette. There were 155 political prisoners and over 600 prisoners of war on the State of Maine when she arrived off George's Island, and many of them were depressed at their first sight of Fort Warren.[6] Colonel Dimick met them at the dock and was dismayed to find the number so much in excess of

[5] U.S. War Dept. (comp.), War of the Rebellion: A Compilation of the Official Records of the Union and Confederate Armies (Washington, 1880-1901), Ser. II, II, 110. Hereafter cited as OR, with all references being to Ser. II. See also Boston Journal, Boston Post, and Daily Evening Traveller, Nov. 1, 1861, Boston Transcript, Nov. 2, 1861.
[6] Fort Warren Register No. 1, Army Section, National Archives. The prisoners—both political and military—are listed on pp. 1-10, 23-61. See also Thomas Sparrow Papers and Diary, Southern Historical Collection, University of North Carolina, entry of Nov. 1, 1861. Hereafter cited as Sparrow Diary.

the 100 he had expected. Unprepared for so many prisoners, he was obliged to tell them they must remain on board another night. The Federal officer in charge of the prisoners from Fort Columbus protested that, owing to the overcrowded conditions on the ship, this delay might have a serious effect on the health of the prisoners. Upon his insistence, four companies from North Carolina were allowed ashore, while the remainder spent an uncomfortable night on the *State of Maine.*[7]

Lieutenant John Buell, the officer assigned to accompany the political prisoners from Fort Lafayette, took this opportunity to consult with them about rooming arrangements. The better known and wealthier among the Confederate soldiers formed into groups of eight or nine for assignment to rooms in the officers' quarters of the fort. Forty-five of the others "who had no money, and for other reasons were not entitled to officers' quarters" were allotted a room seventeen by fifty feet in size. The remainder of the men were lined up the next morning when they disembarked and given their room assignments. Political prisoners were on the south side of the fort, to the left of the archway, and prisoners of war were on the right, or north side.

Almost immediately complaints arose about the arrangements. John M. Brewer, a former reading clerk of the Maryland Legislature, wrote that "there was not a single particle of furniture in my room, except a stove—no chairs, no bedsteads, in a word, nothing." Later in the day Brewer and his roommates were given "two pieces of timber lying parallel with slats nailed transversely theron," but no blankets or mattresses. They discovered that they would have to sleep on these until iron bedsteads arrived from Fort Lafayette. Lawrence Sangston, a Maryland legislator, and seven other men occupied a sixteen-by-eighteen-foot room which, like Brewer's, was unfurnished. Not caring particularly for his roommates, Sangston succeeded in finding a smaller one which he shared with only one other prisoner.[8]

Lack of food was an even more pressing problem. On November 1, Major Thomas Sparrow, one of the North Carolina officers, wrote in his diary that some of the prisoners had missed as many as five meals in succession. Although he himself had had no breakfast, Sparrow felt fortunate by comparison, as he had only gone without three meals.[9] While Brewer was circulating among the rooms (investigating the possibility of a change of quarters), he found many of his fellow prisoners com-

[7] *Ibid.*, entries of Oct. 31–Nov. 1, 1861; John M. Brewer, *Prison Life!* (n.p., 1862), p. 19; Wittiam Gilchrist, *Two Months in Fort Lafayette* (New York, 1862), p. 37; Lawrence Sangston, *The Bastiles of the North* (Baltimore, 1863), pp. 65-66.
[8] Brewer, *Prison Life!*, pp. 19-21; Sangston, *Bastiles of the North*, pp. 66, 79-81; Sparrow Diary, entry of Nov. 1, 1861.
[9] *Idem.*

plaining of their accommodations and the lack of food. He was listening to a speech by a Maryland lawmaker (in which he facetiously referred to his imprisoned colleagues as a traveling committee of the Maryland legislature) when some rations were finally distributed to them. Police Marshal Kane of Baltimore carved a small ham and distributed it around. This meager fare was the first meal at Fort Warren. Obviously, such limited rations were quite inadequate to feed hundreds of men, and Major Sparrow noted that although the officers managed to get something to eat, the enlisted men were not so lucky.[10]

Shortly after they arrived, Confederate officers received a limited parole of the island. In return for their pledge not to attempt an escape, the men had considerable freedom of movement with opportunities for fresh air and exercise. They were not permitted to go near the wharves and barracks. Sangston protested indignantly that the political prisoners were allotted a small outside exercise area only 150 feet long by 30 feet wide, and wondered why there should be discrimination against these men (who had been arrested without any charges being preferred against them) while those captured in arms against the government were allowed so much freedom. However, the Hatteras officers were also dissatisfied; the area where their men were confined was considered part of the barracks and therefore restricted. They complained that this greatly curtailed their freedom of movement because the sentries were unable to distinguish between the prisoners of war and the prisoners of state. They consequently were obliged to obtain permission from the Officer of the Day in order to pass through the cordon from one group to the other.[11]

Boston papers of both political parties carried detailed accounts of the prisoners' arrival at Fort Warren and the subsequent efforts by the Federal government and Bostonians to alleviate the hardships of the situation. A long column in the Boston Post sympathetically described their first hours at the fort and predicted that people in the Boston area would come to their assistance. The Boston Journal reported many of the Hatteras prisoners ill and asked for contributions for their benefit. The Transcript added that the healthy as well as the sick were entitled to consideration. Several days later the Post mentioned a shipment of lumber and iron bedsteads which had been delivered to the fort, and it assured the public that any articles sent there would reach the prisoners.

10 Brewer, Prison Life!, pp. 20-21; John A. Marshall, The American Bastille: A History of Illegal Arrests and Imprisonments during the Civil War (Philadelphia, 1883), p. 113. Hereafter cited as Marshall, American Bastille. See also Willison H. Winder, Secrets of the American Bastille (Philadelphia, 1863), p. 26.

11 Sangston, Bastiles of the North, p. 71; Sparrow Diary, entries of Nov. 2, 6, 1861.

A *Journal* editor urged people to contribute more bedding, and the *Traveller* suggested that donations be forwarded through the mayor's office. On November 6 the *Post* printed an account of a visit to the fort by Mayor Joseph Wightman and again endorsed the drive to aid the prisoners. The mayor's observations confirmed the impression that immediate steps should be taken to ease the situation. He found that the poorer men among the political prisoners had no bedding, the hospital lacked both food and medicines, and the sick were sleeping on the floor with insufficient covering. He described Colonel Dimick as an "excellent officer and kind man" who would "see that anything sent is given to the individual." The mayor also procured clothing, cleaning equipment, blankets, medicines, cocoa, and guava jelly from Evans House, a charitable institution established to aid Union servicemen, and he arranged for the delivery of these goods to the fort.[12]

A month later his efforts in behalf of the prisoners became an election issue in Boston. Republican papers such as the *Transcript* and *Advertiser* assailed the mayor's use of Evans House supplies. The *Traveller* printed a violent attack on Mayor Wightman and, among five reasons for opposing him, cited his aid to "the traitors at Fort Warren" as second in importance. The paper quoted letters of protest from Federal soldiers in Virginia. It made a direct appeal to the Irish vote by reminding its Gaelic readers of Colonel Michael Corcoran's sufferings as a prisoner in Richmond. "Sons of the Emerald Isle," the *Traveller* exhorted, "think of poor Corcoran when you vote on Monday."[13]

Two newspapers came to the mayor's defense. The Boston *Post* asserted that Wightman, in sending the goods to the fort, had acted in a spirit of Christian charity. The Boston *Journal* also supported the Democratic candidate; in one editorial headed "The Transcript on Humanity," it recalled that on November 5 the paper had advocated sending contributions to the prisoners. In another editorial it had referred to the sufferings of the sick at Fort Warren and reminded its readers that the hospital was unable to accommodate them all, that many were obliged to lie on boards, and that Wightman's efforts were specifically in their behalf and not for the political prisoners.[14]

---

[12] Boston *Post*, Nov. 1, 4, 6, Dec. 9, 1861; Boston *Journal,* Nov. 1, 4, 1861; *Daily Evening Traveller,* Nov. 2, 1861; Boston *Transcript,* Nov. 5, Dec. 5, 1861.

[13] Boston *Transcript,* Dec. 5, 1861; Boston *Daily Advertiser,* Dec. 6, 1861; *Daily Evening Traveller,* Dec. 7, 1861.

[14] Boston *Post*, Dec. 7, 1861; Boston *Journal,* Dec. 7, 1861. Despite the charges against him, Wightman was reelected. Yet William Lloyd Garrison's *Liberator,* in reporting the results of the race for mayor, announced that it would have nothing further to say about other charges against Wightman—including the "misdirection of certain charitable donations for our own sick and wounded soldiers for the benefit of the rebel prisoners at Fort Warren." *The Liberator,* Dec. 13, 1861.

After the initial problems attendant upon their arrival had been resolved, the Fort Warren prisoners reported a steady improvement in
their rations, quarters, and in the development of a surprisingly amicable
relationship with the garrison. The quality of the meals was on three
levels. Men with ample means fared excellently; those with not as much
money at their disposal ate reasonably well; their less affluent companions had to be satisfied with regular army rations. Lawrence Sangston
and a group of well-to-do Maryland prisoners formed a private mess
and arranged to purchase various delicacies in Boston. This worked out
very satisfactorily, for Sangston described several culinary triumphs
which made "capital prison fare." His explanatory comment was that
"money will enable you to live anywhere, especially where there is a
Yankee near and he wants it, as he usually does."[15]

While arrangements for this group were being concluded, about 100
North Carolina officers and political prisoners organized a somewhat
less elaborate mess. At a cost of sixteen cents a day, the members were
able to add many items to their army rations of pork and bread. A
released prisoner of war, W. S. S. Andrew, described Major Sparrow's
living conditions to the latter's wife and assured her that he was enjoying good meals. The major wrote her that he, like the other prisoners,
had two meals a day: breakfast at nine and dinner at five. Moreover,
they did not lack variety, for "our closet is never without crackers,
cheese, bologna, sausages,—fruit cake, plain cake—coffee, tea." It is evi-
dent that the food question did not particularly concern him. Sparrow
seemed to have been well supplied; when one of his men gave him a
jar of beef marrow, he made arrangements to send it to his family. On
November 15, set aside by Jefferson Davis as a day of fasting and observed by the Confederate prisoners, no regular meals were served. But
at one o'clock the men appeased their hunger with bread and coffee.[16]

Neither the enlisted men nor the less important political prisoners
fared as well. One of the Maryland contingent said that the North
Carolina men starved for several days after their arrival, but that later
"they received their rations regularly and large boilers were placed in
front of their quarters for them to cook in. These were in the open air,
and not in any way sheltered, and the men had to cook there in all kinds
of weather during the time they remained, which was until they were
exchanged in February, 1862."[17]

Sangston, who visited the North Carolina prisoners in mid-Novem-
ber, wrote: "Each room is furnished with a large iron kettle with a fur-

15 Sangston, *Bastiles of the North*, pp. 71-79.
16 *Ibid.*, p. 73; W.S.S. Andrews to Mrs. Sparrow, Dec. 31, 1861, Sparrow Papers;
Maj. Sparrow to his wife, Dec. 8, 1861, *ibid.*; Sparrow Diary, entry of Nov. 5, 1861.
17 Marshall, *American Bastille*, p. 690.

nace under it outside the door, in which kettle they boil their meat and soup, and make their coffee, all exposed to the weather. I have often noticed them, thinly clad, cooking their rations in a driving rain or snow storm."[18]

A steady influx of gifts helped to make the prisoners more comfortable. Friends and relatives kept them supplied with such comforts as were permitted—as did sympathizers from the border and northern states and charitably inclined Bostonians. Major Sparrow received four shirts and 100 paper collars from a friend in New York, and a Mr. Thomas Simmons of Boston urged the major to call upon him for anything he might need. Colonel William F. Martin of the 7th North Carolina reported to the Confederate Secretary of War that "a friend of Mr. S. Teackly Wallis of Baltimore, a resident of Boston, sent to him some thousand dollars worth of clothing, which he distributed among the sailors and my men." Colonel Martin credited the people of Boston with having given $800 worth of clothing to the Hatteras prisoners.[19]

At least two of the Bostonians who contributed to the prisoners' comfort felt compelled to defend themselves against the charge of being pro-Confederate. Robert C. Winthrop, who had sent wines to ex-Governor Charles S. Morehead of Kentucky and to Charles Faulkner (a former minister to France), and who had also provided overcoats for some of the prisoners, resented such attacks and compared them to Apache ferocity. Referring to charges levied against him, William Appleton expressed the conviction that Christianity and the rules of courtesy justified gifts to his old friends, ex-Minister Faulkner and George Eustis. Moreover, he felt that he had satisfactorily proved his loyalty to the Union by having contributed thousands of dollars to the war effort.[20]

The prisoners at Fort Warren were permitted alcoholic beverages, subject to certain minor restrictions. Lawrence Sangston bought some "Boston whiskey" for three dollars a gallon; because of its poor quality, he declined to purchase more and resolved to wait until his Baltimore friends sent some to him. According to Federal policy, each package received at the fort was examined by an officer. If it contained alcoholic drinks, the contents were rationed out to the prisoner. However, there were special dispensations, for on one occasion Colonel Dimick permitted Sangston to keep a dozen bottles—provided he did not advertise the fact. Dimick's understanding in this matter was evidently appre-

[18] Sangston, *Bastiles of the North*, pp. 84-85.
[19] Sparrow Diary, entry of Nov. 11, 1861; *OR*, III, 763.
[20] R. C. Winthrop, Jr., *A Memoir of Robert C. Winthrop* (Boston, 1897), p. 222; William Appleton, *Selections from the Diaries of William Appleton, 1786-1862* (Boston, 1922), p. 248.

ciated. On at least one occasion, Major Parker shared some whiskey punch with him.[21]

A prisoner's status as an officer or enlisted man determined the comfort of his lodgings, as did social standing among the political prisoners. Shortly after his arrival, Major Sparrow wrote of having a "homelike" bed with paper curtains on the windows and an oilcloth on the table.[22]

The assignment of rooms was a constant source of irritation to both groups. Political prisoners protested that their rooms were overcrowded. Charles Morehead complained of the impossibility of writing letters because he had to share a ten-by-twenty-foot room with nine others. Several weeks later he still professed to be uncomfortable, although there were eight fewer men in his quarters.[23] To protests from guards that the political prisoners were housed better than the garrison was quartered, Colonel Dimick replied that the prisoners were put in the inner two of four similar sets of quarters because they were the safest, and therefore the easiest to guard. Limitations of space necessitated the placing of eight or nine men in each room.[24]

Yet the enlisted men and many of the political prisoners were not as well housed. When Sangston visited the latter to distribute clothing sent by some Baltimore ladies, he found forty-five crowded into a room approximately seventeen by fifty feet. He described it as "almost unendurable" and pervaded by "that peculiar sickening smell known as a 'Poor House Smell' familiar to all who have gone through Almshouses." He soon discovered that the North Carolina enlisted men were even less comfortable. Although their quarters were the same size, the number of occupants varied from sixty-five to eighty-five to the room.[25]

Sangston was more upset than the North Carolinians. One of their number, describing the transfer from Fort Columbus to Fort Warren, wrote that now "we were not so crowded . . . were better fed, and our quarters were greatly improved." Their bunks were three tiers high, wide enough for comfort, and had straw sacks for mattresses. On the same day that Sangston was so disturbed by their plight, the major said they were "cheerful and talk of home." Later in November, he wrote to

[21] Sangston, *Bastiles of the North,* pp. 77-78, 81, 89; Sparrow Diary, entry of Nov. 7, 1861; Samuel A. Green, "Recollections of the Rebellion," Massachusetts Historical Society *Proceedings,* XLVII (1913-14), 186-87.

[22] Sparrow Diary, entry of Nov. 20, 1861.

[23] J. Stoddard Johnston, *Memorial History of Louisville* (Chicago, 1896), I, 194; Mrs. Chapman Coleman, *The Life of John J. Crittenden* (Philadelphia, 1871), II, 333-36.

[24] For example, Charles Faulkner, ex-Governor Morehead and Mayor Brown of Baltimore, along with six others, occupied a room the size of Major Parker's.

[25] Sangston, *Bastiles of the North,* pp. 84-85.

his wife: "The boys have plenty of clothing and are comfortable in all respects."[26]

Christmas of 1861 was a truly festive occasion at the fort. Many gifts for the prisoners arrived in advance of the day, appreciably raising morale. Colonel Dimick was especially understanding and determined that nothing should happen to interfere with the Yuletide celebration. He declined an invitation to spend the holiday in Boston because "among Southern people it was held to be a Christian duty to be royally drunk at Yuletide" and he thought it better to be on hand in case of need. On Christmas Eve he removed the lighting restrictions and notified the men that they might have their lights on as long as they wished. On Christmas Day gifts were opened and the prisoners toasted the good health of friends "over and over." Colonel Dimick was singled out for praise as a "very kind gentleman" who "appears anxious to do all he can to make our time pass off pleasantly."[27]

However, a few instances existed in which war tensions intruded to mar the generally harmonious relationship between Federals and Confederates. On this same Christmas Day, fifteen prisoners attended a mock trial of Secretary of State William H. Seward which was held in one of the casemates. A "judge" and "twelve jurymen" were selected and a dummy representing Seward sat in the box. The trial was short and resulted in a quick verdict of "guilty of treason" in "having abolished the constitution and the laws and ursurped the government." The "execution" was caried out immediately—despite the presence of a Federal officer who was enjoying the trial and a bucket of egg nog simultaneously. On another occasion, Confederate Colonel John Pegram sang "the disloyal song, 'Maryland'." A Union officer, joined by others, followed it immediately with "Vive L' America" and only Pegram's apology for his *faux pas* saved the day.[28]

Both the military and the political prisoners quickly acquired a high degree of respect for Colonel Dimick. John M. Brewer wrote that Dimick "did all in his power to render our condition more tolerable. . . . He was a kind and a good man, and was willing to extend to us every privilege that the Government would allow." Sangston added: "We experienced none of the rudeness and insolence we had daily to encounter at

[26] Theodore B. Hassel to his cousin, Apr. 13, 1864, Cushing B. Hassel Papers, Duke University; Sparrow Diary, entries of Nov. 12, 14, 1861; Maj. Sparrow to his wife, Nov. 14, 1861, Sparrow Papers.

[27] Harry M. Warfield to Charles H. Pitts, Dec. 26, 1861, Pitts Papers, Maryland Historical Society; Charles MacGill to his wife, Dec. 26, 1861, MacGill Papers, Duke University; Sangston, *Bastiles of the North*, pp. 118-19; Francis J. Parker, *The Story of the Thirty-second Regiment* (Boston, 1880), pp. 15-16.

[28] *Ibid.*, pp. 19-20; Sangston, *Bastiles of the North*, pp. 120-21.

Fort Lafayette. . . . In that large heart of his no bitterness, no malice, no sectional hate could find an abiding place. There was not a prisoner under his charge who did not learn to respect and love him before a week had rolled over their heads."[29]

Lieutenant Casey was also well liked, so much so that a group of the North Carolina prisoners presented him with a gold-headed cane when they left the fort. On the other hand, only low opinions existed for the officers of Major Parker's battalion. Sparrow accused them of crowding the entries and making it difficult for the Confederate prisoners to pass. He also remarked that he was glad to be some distance away from their kitchen with its smell of codfish and onions. He was especially critical of Jonathan Pierce of Boston, the commanding officer of Company C. "Foremost among these was (and is) Capt. Pierce, low in stature, stoop shouldered and a low fellow," as well as a "Know Nothing leader."[30]

Early in 1862, shortly after the capture of Forts Henry and Donelson, General G. B. McClellan ordered Confederate Generals Simon Bolivar Buckner and Floyd Tilghman and their field officers sent to Fort Warren.[31] When these men reached Fort Warren in March, they suffered no such hardships as did the first arrivals. In contrast to the stories told by that group, the account of Major Randal W. McGavock was almost enthusiastic. He described the breakfast given the newcomers by the Maryland politicals as the best since his entry into the service. He mentioned sharing a room with four others and, as it was heated by an "anthracite fire" and had an iron cot with a mattress and blanket, McGavock found it "quite comfortable."[32]

Upon the arrival of Buckner and Tilghman at the fort, "Vim," the soldier correspondent of the *Cape Ann Advertiser*, voiced his hope that the two Confederate leaders might be kept in close confinement so as to reflect upon "their crimes against America."[33] By a strange coincidence, the Adjutant General informed Colonel Dimick on the following day that the Secretary of War had ordered the two men restricted to special apartments and denied any contacts except with his permission. Buckner later recalled that when Dimick informed him of the order, the kindly commander had tears in his eyes and Buckner was obliged to con-

[29] *Ibid.*, p. 72; Alexander Hunter, "Confederate Prisoners in Boston," *New England Magazine*, XXIII (1901), 695. See also Richmond *Enquirer*, Aug. 15, 1862.

[30] Sparrow Diary, entry of Dec. 19, 1861; *Daily Evening Traveller*, Dec. 16, 1861; James L. Bowen, *Massachusetts in the War, 1861-1865* (Springfield, 1889), p. 480.

[31] *OR*, III, 269, 275. The Confederate prisoners, then confined at Camp Chase, Ohio, were delighted at any change of scenery. One of the officers described Camp Chase as being so filthy that no self-respecting Tennessee farmer would keep his pigs there. Anrdew J. Allen, "The Diary of Randal William McGavock, 1852-1862" (Unpublished dissertation, George Peabody College 1959), p. 412. Hereafter cited as McGavock Diary.

[32] *Ibid.*, p. 415.   [33] *Cape Ann Advertiser*, Mar. 7, 1862.

sole his warder.[34] About six weeks after this restraining order went into effect, it was modified sufficiently to permit the men to walk on the ramparts for exercise. Yet they did so separately and under guard; furthermore, they were forbidden to speak to their fellow prisoners or to recognize them in any way. The two generals remained in close confinement until late July, 1862, when the restrictions were lifted upon receipt of information that they and their subordinates were to be exchanged. The Richmond *Enquirer* was very critical of this treatment of the "Persecuted" generals and called it the one black spot on Fort Warren's record. G. W. Randolph, the Confederate Secretary of War, said of Buckner's imprisonment that "with the exception of denying him intercourse with the other prisoners, he was kindly treated, well lodged, and allowed to take air on the ramparts. . . . As we exercised the right of separating prisoners, we cannot call in question that of the enemy to do the same thing."[35]

There was no overcrowding in 1862, and most of the Fort Donelson prisoners were satisfied with their room assignments. Colonel H. C. Lockhart wrote that the fort was "elegantly built as to comfort" and that the apartments given the prisoners were neat, spacious, and comfortable. His room was eighteen by twenty feet, light and airy, with a fireplace and a washroom, and he shared it with three officers and a political prisoner. Dr. Charles Macgill, a Maryland legislator, had only five other men in his quarters. The prisoner exchange of July 31 still further reduced the numbers rooming together.[36]

Neither were there any serious complaints about bedding from this group. The first ones to arrive at the fort were satisfied with their folding cots, shuck mattresses, and blankets. The accounts of some of those who followed imply that their sleeping arrangements were not comfortable although they apparently were no worse than those provided for the Federal garrison. J. H. Tomb, a chief engineer in the Confederate Navy, wrote that in his quarters in the casemates the prisoners slept on bunks which consisted of pine boards "three in a row" and that straw and a blanket apiece were issued to them. Lieutenant Alexander Hunter spoke of bunks built one over the other and the usual one blanket. None of these men sounded at all disturbed about their accommodations.[37]

Similarly, complaints about the rations were few during 1862. The newcomers fitted easily into the established routine. Major McGavock

[34] *OR*, III, 355; Nashville *Banner*, Dec. 11, 1909.

[35] Richmond *Enquirer*, Aug. 15, 1862; *OR*, IV, 804.

[36] H. C. Lockhart to his wife, May 11, 1862, Lockhart Letters, Southern Historical Collection, University of North Carolina; Charles MacGill to his wife, Apr. 9, 15, 1862, MacGill Papers.

[37] H. C. Lockhart to his wife, Apr. 5, May 18, 1862, Lockhart Letters; J. H. Tomb, "Prison Life at Fort Warren, Boston Harbor," *Confederate Veteran*, XXI (1913), 110; Hunter, "Confederate Prisoners in Boston," p. 694.

joined the Baltimore mess, which he rated as highly as the meals in any
first class hotel in the country. Lockhart spoke of eating well for $2.50 a
week. John Wilkinson of the Confederate Navy wrote that when the
meals were served, each officer took his turn carving or waiting on
tables. Commodore Barron was "graceful and accomplished" and "shone
conspicuous as a carver," while colonels, majors, and captains, with
spotless napkins on their arms, anticipated the guests' every wish.[38]

This time also, friends and sympathizers generously supplied the
prisoners with gifts. Lieutenant Hunter, for example, received packages
from New York and Boston in addition to those from the South. According to him, some "Rebel Sympathizers" from Boston attempted to visit
Fort Warren. When they failed, they showed their colors by supplying
the Confederates with gray uniforms. He added that so many gifts of
food, books, and clothing were received during this period that the prisoners shared the contents of various packages with their guards.[39]

There were no prisoners at Fort Warren from the latter part of 1862
until July, 1863. In December, 1861, and February, 1862, virtually all
of the North Carolina prisoners were sent South to be exchanged; in
July of the latter year, the Fort Donelson officers were similarly returned.
Various methods of adjudication were used in connection with the
political prisoners. Some were released after taking the oath of allegiance, others were freed on parole, and on November 26, 1862, the last
small group of obstinate holdouts among them were unconditionally
set free by the Federal government.

Late in 1863, Colonel Dimick was transferred from his assignment for
reasons of health. Prisoners sent to Fort Warren during the latter part of
the war were not as comfortable under Dimick's successor, Major Stephen Cabot. Edward A. Pollard, the Confederate editor who was captured on a blockade runner, stated that the rooms were badly overcrowded, that 160 men lived in a section of the fort nicknamed "the gunboat" and that they were "packed in three apartments," each "fifteen by
sixteen feet." Lieutenant T. K. Porter of the *Florida* claimed that eleven
newly arrived officers were put into a room (fifty by eighteen feet) with
thirty-two other prisoners. Major Stephen Cabot asserted that "the case-
mate occupied by Captain Webb and his officers, 29 in all, is of the same
dimensions as occupied by 40 of our troops."[40]

[38] McGavock Diary, p. 446; H. C. Lockhart to his wife, May 11, 1862, Lockhart
Letters; John Wilkinson, *The Narrative of a Blockade Runner* New York, 1877),
p. 70.

[39] Hunter, "Confederate Prisoners in Boston," pp. 695-96.

[40] Edward A. Pollard, *Observations in the North* (Richmond, 1865), pp. 42-43;
OR, VI, 1024; T. K. Porter, "Capture of the Confederate Steamer Florida by the
U.S. Steamer Wachusett," *Southern Historical Society Papers*, XII (1884), 43. Here-
after cited as *SHSP*.

All beds and bedding provided at the fort at this time were of the type common to the poorer class of prisoners during Colonel Dimick's command.[41] Moreover, from this period until the end of hostilities, complaints about the food increased. Pollard, who had a tendency to overdramatize, referred to his rations as "the diaphanous slices of bread and the bits of fat pork." Some prisoners found that their rations of fourteen ounces of bread, eight ounces of cooked meat, and half a pint of soup on three days, and two potatoes, with some beans or hominy on the other days, were by careful apportioning, "enough to appease their hunger"; but others "were hungry all the time." Harry Gilmor also thought the rations inadequate and wrote: "It was difficult to make our scanty fare hold out, and two-thirds of the time I went to bed hungry."[42]

Major Cabot, in referring to this dissatisfaction with the food, conceded that "there have been complaints that [the prisoners] have not a sufficiency of bread." He then offered the somewhat improbable explanation: "I find the bread is so good that some eat more than their allowance, 18 oz., and this may deprive others of their full share."[43]

The prisoners resented new rulings in regard to their dealings with the sutlers. Those who could afford it were prevented from purchasing foodstuffs, such as sugar and coffee, to share with comrades who had less cash. General Adam R. Johnson actually enjoyed his convalescence from a bad fall, as the post physician authorized him to buy various foods which otherwise would not have been permitted him. The Federal policy toward gifts also underwent a change. In the summer of 1864, before restrictions went into effect, Pollard received several letters and packages of food from friends in Boston. Gilmor, however, was disappointed somewhat later when he learned that he was not allowed to receive food, while General Johnson was irritated to discover that friends behind the Union lines and in Boston "made efforts to supply me" with food but the packages were refused at the fort.[44]

None of the subsequent commanders at Fort Warren made such an impression on the prisoners as did Colonel Dimick, although the men apparently bore them no ill will. Even Pollard, who was often vindictive in his remarks, wrote that after he was registered by Major Cabot on

---

[41] For example, see Pollard, *Observations in the North*, p. 33; Harry Gilmor, *Four Years in the Saddle* (New York, 1866), pp. 287-88, 290.

[42] *Ibid.*, p. 289; Pollard, *Observations in the North*, pp. 33-34; *SHSP*, XII (1884), 43.

[43] *OR*, VI, 1024. In another report Cabot stated derisively: "They consume the entire allowance and complain that they do not get enough to eat." "Auxiliary Register No. 4, Military Prison at Fort Warren," Army Section, National Archives.

[44] *SHSP*, XII (1884), 43; Adam R. Johnson, *The Partisan Rangers of the Confederate States Army* (Louisville, 1904), pp. 198-99; Pollard, *Observations in the North*, pp. 42-43; Gilmor, *Four Years in the Saddle*, p. 289.

his arrival, he was turned over to Lieutenant Edward Parry, who was "very civil" and spared him "the indignity of a search" of his effects. According to Pollard the fort's officers showed the prisoners "all the kindness they could venture within the framework of the system of *punishment* of prisoners of war demanded at Washington." Prison officials were also sympathetic with the natural desire of the men for freedom. They often made a point of recommending the release of those who made application to the Commissary General of Prisoners.[45]

When the war ended, the prisoners, next to their primary concern about the South's future, were greatly interested in the relaxation of the conditions of their confinement pending their release. Once again they were permitted to receive gifts. Lieutenant General Richard S. Ewell, captured at Sayler's Creek, described his rations to his sister as "bread and meat, occasionally baked beans or grits" and then told her she might now send him a package of choicer food to supplement this diet.[46]

Relations between officers of both factions seemed as harmonious as in former years except for one unfortunate instance of sectional bias. General Eppa Hunton of Lee's staff was contemptuous of Major Harvey A. Allen, the fort's commander at that time, because in spite of his North Carolina origin, Allen had remained with the Union. The Confederate prisoners "never recognized him" and refused to shake hands with him on their departure. Hunton conceded that the officers and men at Fort Warren were kind to him. He made the interesting observation that the Confederate generals first learned that they were to be freed when the troops of the garrison cheered upon hearing the news.[47]

As orders came from Washington directing the release of different categories of prisoners, newspaper reports of their departure were inevitably colored by some of the animosity of the conflict. Both the *Traveller* and the *Journal* stated that they spoke well of their treatment and presented a favorable contrast to Federal soldiers who survived Libby Prison and Andersonville. The *Advertiser* noted: "Their condition did not indicate any lack of good living, and widely differed from that of many who return from Southern prisons."[48]

The Fort Warren Register at the National Archives, which ordinarily

[45] Pollard, *Observations in the North*, pp. 32-33. Summaries of those Fort Warren prisoners who made such applications are in the Case Histories of the Commissary General of Prisoners, Army Section, National Archives.

[46] Percy G. Hamlin (ed.), *The Making of a Soldier* (Richmond, 1935), pp. 134-35. The incarceration at Fort Warren of Confederate Vice President A. H. Stephens and Postmaster General John H. Reagan, while not told here, may be found in their autobiographies.

[47] Eppa Hunton, *Autobiography of Eppa Hunton* (Richmond, 1933), p. 139.

[48] *Daily Evening Traveller*, June 12, 1865; Boston *Journal*, June 12, 1865; Boston *Daily Advertiser*, June 14, 1865.

recorded only the basic facts about individual prisoners, departed from custom to point out that only twelve deaths occurred there during the war. This is a real tribute to the unusually good conditions and absence of serious hardship. Despite the later decline in comfort, the character of Fort Warren during the Civil War was the reflection of the character of Colonel Dimick. Even without the obvious comparisons with contemporary military prisons, his influence and sympathy made this New England fortress an outstanding example of humanity in time of stress.

ROCK ISLAND PRISON BARRACKS

T. R. Walker

One of the westernmost Confederate prisoner-of-war camps was located on Rock Island, a government-owned island in the Mississippi River between Davenport, Iowa, and Rock Island and Moline, Illinois. In the frontier era from 1816 to 1836, Fort Armstrong stood on the western tip of this island, and for the past century the plot of land has been widely known as the site of Rock Island Arsenal. Constructed in mid-1863, the Rock Island prison camp received its first prisoners in December of that same year. In the months that followed, the camp quickly gained a mixed reputation—to some it was a Northern "Andersonville"; to others it offered more than the necessary comforts.

On July 14, 1863, Captain Charles A. Reynolds of the Quartermaster Department received orders from Quartermaster General M. C. Meigs to construct a depot for prisoners of war at Rock Island. The Commissary General of Prisons furnished construction plans, which called for the erection of eighty-four prisoners' barracks and a rough board fence to enclose them. Construction began during the last of August, 1863; two months later the camp stood ready to receive its first contingent of prisoners.[1]

Each barracks building was 100 feet long, 22 feet wide, and 12 feet high; all barracks faced eastward. Each barracks had twelve windows, two doors, and two roof ventilators, four feet long and two feet wide. The kitchen for each building was located at the west end and separated from the sleeping quarters by a wall located eighteen feet from the west end. The remaining eighty-two feet were taken up by living and sleeping quarters. Sixty double bunks were constructed, enabling each barracks to house 120 prisoners. There were six rows with fourteen barracks in each row. The buildings were thirty feet apart and, with one exception, faced onto streets 100 feet wide. The fourth row opened on an avenue 130 feet wide—one of two avenues bisecting the prison.

SGT. T. R. WALKER *is Curator of the John M. Browning Memorial Museum at the Rock Island Arsenal and, as such, is eminently qualified to recount the story of this island-prison.*

[1] U.S. War Dept. (comp.) *War of the Rebellion: A Compilation of the Official Records of the Union and Confederate Armies* (Washington, 1880-1901), Ser. II, VI, 115, 281, 634, 663, 938, 948. Hereafter cited as *OR;* all references are to Ser. II.

The barracks were enclosed by a stockade fence 1,300 feet long, 900 feet wide, and 12 feet high. A board walk was constructed on the outside of the fence, four feet from the top, and sentry boxes were placed every 100 feet. Double-gate sally ports located on the east and west ends of the fence afforded the only openings into the enclosure. A strong guardhouse was erected outside the fence at each of the two gates.[2]

The Commissary General of Prisoners, Colonel William Hoffman, made an inspection of the empty prison in November, 1863. Just a few days before Colonel Hoffman's trip, a large fire destroyed several of the prison barracks in Camp Douglas, near Chicago, Illinois. Colonel Hoffman, in his report to the Secretary of War, stated his intention of transferring 1,000 prisoners left without shelter at Camp Douglas to Rock Island Prison Barracks.

This transfer did not occur until December, 1863, when 5,592 prisoners—most of whom were captured by Grant's army at Lookout Mountain and Missionary Ridge—arrived at Rock Island. A great deal of suffering characterized this first group. They were far from their homes; moreover, the coldness of the climate had left them half-frozen, for on the day of their arrival the temperature dropped to thirty-two degrees below zero. This condition was aggravated at the very outset by an epidemic of dreaded smallpox. Prison doctors found ninety-four cases of this disease in the group, and all had been exposed to it.

The prison surgeon in charge, Dr. J. J. Temple; his aged assistant, Surgeon T. J. Iles; and Dr. Marcellus Moxley were faced with the responsibility of checking this terrible disease without hospital wards or adequate medicines. According to a February, 1864, report made by Assistant Surgeon General A. M. Clark, Dr. Temple was not aware of the extent of his authority or duties as a surgeon in charge; Dr. Iles, although skilled professionally, was completely bewildered; and Dr. Moxley was a very young officer, anxious to do his duty but entirely unfitted both by temperament and experience for a charge of such magnitude.[3]

During his inspection of the prison, Surgeon Clark found thirty-eight cases of smallpox which had not been reported to the commanding officer by the surgeon in charge. Moreover, these men had been lying in bunks among the healthy. Neither had the provost marshal reported these cases, although they should have come to his attention in the daily inspections that he was supposed to have made. Surgeon Clark laid a large part of blame for this smallpox epidemic on those officers at the Louisville, Kentucky, prison who allowed prisoners to be sent to Rock Island Prison Barracks, even though they had been exposed to this con-

[2] Ibid., VIII, 993.   [3] Ibid., VI, 938.

tagious disease—with some already broken out. Although the officers at Louisville denied any responsibility on their part, the extent of the disease and the advanced stages of the ninety-four cases contradicted this denial. Dr. Clark, on finding the vaccine nearly exhausted, immediately wired for a sufficient supply and directed its immediate use on arrival.

Since no hospital at this time had been erected, Surgeon Clark requested that certain barracks in the southwest section of the stockade be used as hospital wards. He also directed that pest houses be erected on the south shore of the island about a half-mile from the prison.

By the end of December, ninety-four prisoners had died and had been buried about 400 yards directly south of the prison. In January, 1864, 231 prisoners died; in February, the toll rose to 346.[4]

Surgeon Clark thought the site of the burials to be too close to the prison and directed the use of a more distant site on the south shore of the island. This area, however, could not be used because of the depth of the soil was found to be too shallow. The present site of the Confederate Cemetery, located about 1,000 yards southeast of the prison stockade, was then decided upon. The 671 burials in the original site were removed to the new cemetery by the middle of March, 1864; all Confederate dead after March 1 were buried in the new location. Union soldiers succumbing to the same diseases as the prisoners were buried on a site about 100 yards northwest of the Confederate Cemetery.[5]

During the twenty months that prisoners were confined at Rock Island, 1,960 died from various diseases. No record exists of deaths occurring from wounds. In the same period, 171 Union soldiers stationed as guards died of disease or exposure suffered while on duty. The Union dead not later claimed by relatives were reinterred in the present Rock Island National Cemetery on the island.

In February, 1864, the first evidence of friction between the prison command and Rock Island Arsenal command was recorded. Though Congress had, as of July 11, 1862, authorized the construction of an arsenal on the island, it was not until October, 1863, that construction actually began. Major Charles P. Kingsbury of the Ordnance Department was ordered to take charge of the erection of the arsenal buildings. On February 26, 1864, he wrote Captain Reynolds that Reynold's teamsters, in the work of hauling supplies and material to the prison, had not kept to the road, had broken down fences around the arsenal construction area, and were driving the wagons at will over the lower (west) end of the island. On March 16, Kingsbury wrote to the Chief of Ordnance, General George D. Ramsay, concerning the cutting of trees

[4] *Ibid.*, p. 1002.
[5] Survey Map of Rock Island, 1865, John M. Browning Memorial Museum, Rock Island Arsenal. The Federal cemetery is now a part of number fourteen fairway of the Rock Island Arsenal Golf Course.

by men in the prison command. Kingsbury requested that orders be issued to that command before more trees were removed or any buildings erected. The following day, he again informed the Chief of Ordnance that the Davenport House on the island was being used by the prison command and requested that its occupants be ordered to turn the house over to the Ordnance Department. Subsequent letters from Kingsbury bore complaints of prison guards restricting Ordnance workmen from proceeding with their work, of the firing of muskets by the guard, of driving laborers from the stone quarry in which they were working, and even of the writer's being stopped from crossing over the river to the island on the railroad bridge from his home in Davenport. This friction existed to some degree throughout the entire period that the prison was in operation.[6]

Though the prison had previously come under inspections from Colonel Hoffman, General William W. Orme, and Medical Inspector N. S. Townshend, it is from the reports of Assistant Surgeon General Clark that a clear description of prison conditions may be obtained.[7] To Surgeon Clark must go much of the credit in directing the necessary changes needed in checking smallpox and other diseases and for putting into operation the sanitation system that made life for prisoners more bearable.

Surgeon Clark's stay at the prison extended from February 10 to March 4, 1864. Through his efforts, plans for a suitable hospital for non-contagious diseases were drawn up, and this hospital was eventually erected on the site of the present arsenal shops. Pest houses were erected on the south shore of the island; all soldiers or prisoners suffering from smallpox had been removed to these buildings by March 1, 1864. The ten barracks at the southwest corner of the prison in which the diseased soldiers had been quartered were thoroughly cleaned and given an interior coating of whitewash. They were then used as non-contagious disease wards until the hospital for such cases was erected. The sewage system was constructed for better drainage and sanitation. Surgeon Clark had the water supply system altered so that adequate water could be made available to everyone in the camp.

Food was rationed in bulk by the Quartermaster Department; prisoners of each barracks received rations for a period of ten days. Clark found no inspections being made of the food after it was issued, but he adjudged the rations to be sufficient in quantity.[8] Clark found the prisoners exceptionally clean, though the clothing supply was insufficient. Prisoners were allowed clothing sent by relatives, and the government issued clothing almost daily when supplies were available.

[6] Correspondence in Rock Island Arsenal Ledger, Browning Museum.
[7] For example, see *OR*, VI, 938-48.   [8] *Ibid.*, VIII, 17.

Surgeon W. Watson of the U.S. Volunteers relieved Dr. Moxley as Post Surgeon on March 4, 1864. About two weeks later—in a letter to the commanding officer—Watson stated the need for a larger hospital and increased issues of clothing for the convalescents from the smallpox wards. He deplored the critical conditions existing in the ten prison barracks then being used as hospital wards. The crowded condition did not permit classification in arranging patients, which would have enabled the medical staff to guard against contagious diseases. Watson stated that he had separated most of the cases of erysipelas which, before the erection of the last smallpox wards on the south shore of the island, had been compelled to remain wherever they occurred, spreading the disease to patients around them. He endeavored to set aside one of the wards for the reception of new cases from the barracks where the existence of smallpox was suspected, but was not permitted to do so. Instead, he was compelled to leave the diseased cases among the healthy prisoners until the appearance of eruptions dispelled all doubts.[9]

Special arrangements for feeding severely sick prisoners of proper diet were completely lacking. Watson's report to Surgeon Charles Tripler late in March was alarming in content. On the March 4 morning sick report, Watson stated, 350 prisoners were sick in quarters and 714 were in the hospital. Of the latter, 420 were in smallpox wards, and at one period 485 cases of smallpox were crowded into a space which should have accommodated only 240 cases. Surgeon Tripler was also aware that in the preceding three months 671 prisoners had died. He was therefore doubly alarmed upon receiving Watson's report. He enclosed this report in a letter to the acting Surgeon General, Joseph K. Barnes, and stated that he was instructing Surgeon Watson to use all measures necessary to control the epidemic. He also requested the War Department to resume construction of the hospital, which had been stopped by orders from Colonel Hoffman.[10]

In accordance with these instructions, Watson was to build a suitable laundry; the clothing of all smallpox patients was to be burned; and the privilege of requesting issues of necessary articles would be extended to the prisoners. Surgeon Tripler ordered Robert W. Burnet of the Cincinnati Sanitation Commission immediately to send 150 suits of clothing to the smallpox patients so that the burning process could be started at once. Yet the epidemic raged on, reaping 283 more deaths during the month of March. The War Department, with the facts finally laid before it, countermanded Colonel Hoffman's directive suspending the erection of the hospital and ordered its immediate completion.

Surgeon Clark, in an April, 1864, inspection, made a report on the contagious disease hospital (pest houses). This group of buildings was lo-

9 Ibid., VI, 1022; VII, 14.   10 Ibid., VII, 12.

cated at the foot of the present Gillespie Avenue on the south shore of
the island. Clark described these buildings as six in number, each 150
feet long, 24 feet wide, and 12 feet high. Additional buildings consisted of a laundry, guardhouse, dead house, and a building housing the
dispensary and storerooms, as well as rooms for attendants and nurses.
The laundry had two forty-gallon boilers which were kept busy boiling
the clothing of the patients. Two old houses adjacent to the pest houses
were used for the reception of smallpox patients: one for prisoners, the
other for the troops.[11] That same month witnessed a marked decrease
in both the death rate and the number of severe smallpox cases. Many
new cases appeared in milder form and the recovery rate rose sharply.

The prison's non-contagious disease hospital, when completed, had a
capacity of 560 beds in fourteen wards. Later a post hospital was erected
for non-contagious disease patients among the troops. Other buildings
constructed in the early part of 1864 were the administration building,
officers' quarters, guardhouses, and barracks for the troops.[12]

For a time, members of the 37th Iowa Invalid Corps were stationed as
guards at the prison.[13] Six companies were quartered for a time in the
city of Rock Island and then transferred to six prison barracks within
the stockade. This situation existed until barracks for the regiment were
erected in 1864.

Captain Reynolds, busy constructing sewers and waterworks for the
prison, requested the use of prisoners in pushing the work forward.
Since they would be doing the work of civilians, they could expect some
sort of compensation.

Colonel A. J. Johnson, the prison commandant, on forwarding Captain Reynold's request to Colonel Hoffman, recommended that these
prisoner laborers receive forty cents a day. Yet Colonel Hoffman, in his
endorsement to the Secretary of War, recommended that the pay be set
at ten cents per day for mechanics and five cents for laborers. This recommendation was approved by the Chief of Staff, General Halleck. All
labor was on a voluntary basis, and the pay was credited to the individual prisoner's account in the prison sutler's store and could be drawn
on as desired.[14]

Rising a short distance south of the prison walls was a natural bluff
which extended eastward from the prison. On this ridge Captain Reynolds built a reservoir. Its height above the prison gave its water enough

---

[11] *Ibid.*, p. 23. These old houses were probably erected during the squatters' invasion of Rock Island in 1857.

[12] *Ibid.*, p. 27.

[13] Composed of men too old for the conscription law, the 37th Iowa contained
428 men over the age of fifty, 145 in their sixties, and one man, Curtis King of Mus-
catine, who was eighty.

[14] *OR*, VII, 180.

54

force when released to flush out the sewers, and furnished enough pressure through pipe lines to hydrants located at various places to fight fires in any buildings of the garrison or prison. The reservoir had a capacity of 1,800,000 gallons, the water being fed into it by a pump located east of the reservoir and upstream from the buildings. An open sewer, lined with masonry stone, was dug from the reservoir through the south and north walls of the prison down the center of the main avenue. This sewer was built in such a manner that, when the water gate at the reservoir was opened, the water would flush all waste out into the river. This water gate also allowed a continuous flow of water to a depth of three or four inches. At the point where the sewer ditch passed under the walls of the prison, large bars of iron were driven into the ground to prevent it becoming an escape route. Smaller lateral sewers from the east and west sides of this sewer were excavated so that all sewage was channeled into the main sewer. Laundries, wash houses, and privies were built over this sewer. Yet this system did not go into full use until the middle of January, 1865.[15]

The life of any prisoner of war at best is very monotonous; this was certainly the case at Rock Island Prison. Prisoners passed their time in making trinkets of shells and other materials, which were sold for whatever price they could obtain. Plots of escape were many, yet only forty-one escapees managed to elude recapture.[16] On June 14, 1864, ten of the prisoners tried their luck by tunneling from under Barracks No. 42 and then under the south wall. The last two prisoners coming up out of the tunnel were discovered by the sentry and the alarm was sounded. Guards hurried out and captured three prisoners on the island. Another drowned while attempting to swim the south channel of the Mississippi River (which was about 400 feet wide). The remaining six crossed the river without being caught and made their way over a high ridge which separates the Mississippi and Rock rivers. Four were captured near the latter stream, but two made good their escape.

The troops making up the garrison at the prison consisted of the 4th Regiment, U.S. Veterans Reserve Corps; the 37th Iowa Volunteer Regiment (The Greybeards); the 48th Iowa (100-day men)—three companies of the 2nd Battalion; 133rd Illinois (100-day men); 197th Pennsylvania Volunteers; and the 108th U.S. Regiment Colored Infantry. This last group arrived for duty at the prison on September 23, 1864.

Just a month had passed when on the night of October 24, 1864, John P. McClanahan, prisoner of war living in Barracks No. 8, was shot to

---

15 *Ibid.*, VI, 1003.

16 One of this fortunate few was William O. Wynn, who later recounted his experiences in *Biographical Sketch of the Life of an Old Confederate Soldier* (Greenville, Texas, 1916).

death in an attempt to escape under the north wall of the prison. Mc-
Clanahan, a private in Company D, 9th Tennessee Cavalry, was shot
at 1:30 p.m. by the sentry at Post 13, Private Peter Cowherd, C Company, 108th U.S. Colored Infantry. A commission consisting of Captains
J. G. Robinson and B. R. Wagner and First Lieutenant M. F. Bishop was
ordered to convene at 3 p.m., October 25, to inquire into the shooting.
After all evidence was presented, Private Cowherd was acquitted, his
act being considered in the performance of his duty.[17]

On being informed of President Lincoln's Amnesty Proclamation of
December 8, 1863, many prisoners took the oath of allegiance. This enabled them to enlist in the Union forces but only upon assurance that
they would be assigned to garrisons in the West. Yet this measure was
far from an emancipation. In mid-December Colonel Johnson, the
prison commander, reported a total of 1,797 prisoner-enlistees crowded
into sixteen barracks. Moreover, being no longer prisoners but ostensible
soldiers of the U.S. army, the men could not be issued clothing from the
prison stock. Since they had not been officially organized into authorized
companies, neither could they obtain issues from the Quartermaster.
Colonel Johnson sent urgent but unanswered appeals to the Provost
Marshal General, under whose directions these recruits had been mustered, asking for their removal to some camp of organization such as
Camp Butler or Camp Fry in Illinois.

The response to the Amnesty Proclamation among Rock Island's prisoners was so great that a group of Confederates still loyal to the Southern cause felt it their duty to use every means within their power to
counteract this defection to the enemy. These men frantically began re-
enlisting prisoners into Confederate military service. The plan was put
into effect on January 7, 1864. Loyal Confederates recruited fellow prisoners only for the cavalry, which was the only arm in which most were
willing to serve a new tour. This recruiting continued throughout the
year, with prisoner recruits being formed into companies of 130 men
each. On February 9, 1865, a petition was drawn up and signed by ten
prison petitioners and sent to President Jefferson Davis. In their petition,
the prisoners stated they had re-enlisted about 1,300 men. As would be
expected, this component never saw active duty.[18]

Beginning late in 1864, the reputation of the Confederate prison on
Rock Island was likened to that of Andersonville in the South. This ad-
verse publicity started when several articles appeared in a local newspaper. Not until a story was published in the Rock Island *Argus* of No-

[17] *OR*, VII, 1037. McClanahan's remains occupy Grave No. 1584 in the island's
Confederate Cemetery.
[18] *Ibid.*, VIII, 201.

vember 21, 1864, did Colonel Johnson bother to reply. The issue of that
date spurred the Colonel to a long and bitter retort:

Mr. Editor: In your issue of the 21st instant I notice an Article on the
treatment of prisoners of war at this depot. Up to this time I have passed
unnoticed the numerous erroneous articles that have appeared in the papers
of this vicinity in relation to the occurrences at this post, but in this case
I will deviate from an established rule and give your article of the 21st
instant the notice it seems to merit. Owing to the fact that your paper has
a wide circulation among the relatives of a large number of the prisoners,
it is desirable that the antidote should quickly follow the poison in order
to save the wives, mothers, fathers, sisters, and brothers of the prisoners
unnecessary grief. Your assertions are founded on what you term a talk
with several newly made Union men, and it would be difficult to imagine
it possible to put together a greater amount of error and misrepresentation
in the same space.

You start with an issue of eight ounces of bread and a small piece of
salt meat the size of two fingers daily, give large numbers the scurvy and
deliberately and willfully torture them to death, and call for fearful judgment
on the guilty parties. Did you not blush when you published in your issue
of the 22nd instant the official report of the deaths of prisoners at this
depot, amounting to three for the previous week? That report was a scorching answer to your whole article of the 21st instant.

On the 1st of June last the issue of rations to prisoners was reduced to
the following: Pork or bacon, ten ounces (in lieu of fresh beef); fresh beef,
fourteen ounces; flour or soft bread, sixteen ounces; hard bread, fourteen
ounces (in lieu of flour or soft bread); corn-meal, sixteen ounces (in lieu
of flour or soft bread); beans or peas, twelve pounds and a half to 100 rations;
rice or hominy, eight pounds to 100 rations; soap, four pounds to 100 rations; salt, three pounds and a quarter to 100 rations; vinegar, three quarts
to 100 rations. The bread and meat issue is two ounces per day less than
is issued to the troops. The prisoners have no labor to perform while the
troops are worked hard. When prisoners are worked they do so voluntarily,
and receive additional rations and also pay. Hundreds of dollars are ex-
pended every month to purchase tobacco to distribute among them. They
have always been allowed to receive necessary clothing from their relatives,
and scarcely a day passes without a large number of the most needy are
brought out to receive clothing furnished by the Government. Thousands
of suits of clothes, and likewise of blankets, have been issued, and the Government furnishes more clothing to destitute prisoners in one day than
friends do in two months. Only about one-fifth of the prisoners have received clothing from friends, while the other four-fifths are supplied entirely
by the Government, and as a general thing that one-fifth are rebels and are
supplied by rebels and rebel sympathizers.

The above issue of rations is made to the letter. Each company of prisoners
receives ten days at a time, in bulk, they having the entire control of the
distribution among themselves, and the few Union prisoners in each company are at the mercy of a rebel majority. That, perhaps, will account, if
true, for the eight ounces of bread and the small piece of meat received by
them.

Did it ever occur to you that, while you can spend the necessary time to pen an article like that and use nearly a column of your paper for its publication, your files may be searched in vain for the smallest editorial paragraph in condemnation of the rebel authorities for the brutal treatment of our men in their hands? You seem to be in doubt as to whom belongs the treatment of the prisoners at this depot. I will enlighten you. The treatment of them here and all issues to them are made strictly in accordance with orders from the War Department. I will embrace this opportunity to state that by a perusal of the columns of the *Argus* for the past year I am enabled to form a correct opinion of your position, and I have no objection to give you, in plain terms, what would be my action in regard to the treatment of prisoners in my charge if discretionary power rested with me: In the first place, instead of placing them in fine, comfortable barracks, with three large stoves in each and as much coal as they can burn both day and night, I would place them in one with no shelter but the heavens, as our poor men were at Andersonville.

Instead of giving them the same quality and nearly the same quantity of provisions that the troops on duty receive, I would give them, as near as possible, the same quantity and quality of provisions that the fiendish rebels give our men; and instead of a constant issue of clothing to them, I would let them wear their rags, as our poor men in the hands of the rebel authorities are obliged to do; or, in other words, had I the power, strict retaliation would be practiced by me. Again, if discretionary power rested with me, I would arrest and confine the known sympathizers with the rebellion residing in Rock Island and Davenport, and quite a large number would be quickly added to our list of prisoners, and those communities would be relieved from a more dangerous element than open rebels in arms.[19]

Colonel Johnson also found it necessary to defend his prison camp early the following year. In several letters to the War Department, he branded as completely untrue a story that appeared in the January 3, 1865, issue of the New York *Daily News*. Written by an alleged visitor to the compound, and headed "Prisoners at Rock Island—Inhuman Treatment—They Feed on Dogs and Rats," the article stated:

The conditioning and suffering of the rebel prisoners at Rock Island is a source of agony to every heart not absolutely dead to the feelings of common humanity and the scantiest Christian Mercy. There are from 6,000 to 8,000 confined there. Many have taken "the oath," any oath, to save themselves from actual starvation. These released prisoners, though liberated at different intervals of time, all tell the same story. The allowance to each man has been one small loaf of bread (it takes three to make a pound) and a piece of meat, two inches square, per day. This was the ration. Lately it has been reduced. Think of it—reduced! All the released ones say that no man can live on the rations given, and that there are men who would do anything to get enough to eat. Such is the wretched, ravenous condition of these poor starving creatures that several dogs which have come to the barracks with teams have fallen victims to their hunger, and they are trapping rats and mice for food, actually to save life. Many of them are nearly naked,

[19] *Ibid.*, pp. 16-17.

barefooted, bareheaded, and without bed-clothes; exposed to ceaseless torture from the chill and pitiless winds of the Upper Mississippi. Thus naked and hungry, and in prison, enduring a wretchedness which no tongue can describe, no language tell, they suffer from day to day, each day their number growing less by death; death, their only comforter, their only merciful visitor.

God in heaven! Shall these things continue? Can we hope for success in our cause? Will a merciful and just God bless and prosper it if such cruel inhumanity is practiced by our rulers? May we not provoke a terrible and just chastisement at His hands? No Christian heart, knowing the facts, can feel otherwise. Many charitable persons, influenced by no other motives than common humanity and Christian duty, have sent supplies of clothing to these prisoners, but they have not been permitted to reach them. I have heard of sales of such clothing having been made across the river in Davenport at very low prices. Is it possible that the authorities at Washington know of and approve these things?

A good many have taken the oath, stating afterwards to citizens that they did so really to save them from starvation. I learn that there are about 5,000 confined here who have resolved to die rather than do so. Although they are wrong, is there not a sublime heroism in the adherence of these men, amid such trials, to a cause which they believe to be right.[20]

After the war a Confederate prisoner related some of his experiences at Rock Island in an article for the Louisville *Age*. "In the better days of life there," he wrote, "the bill of fare was generous—coffee, sugar, rice, molasses, boiled meats, and bread in the loaf. After the Andersonville excitement, rations were reduced and the state of affairs began to be painful. A wicked commissary tried a little private retaliation and corn beef got to be abominable." As to the treatment of prisoners, he reflected, "various punishments were devised against those caught in rebellious ways—riding a rail, hanging by the thumbs, wearing a ball and chain, etc., but on the whole the Federal government was liberal."[21]

In the twenty-month existence of Rock Island Prison, a total of 12,409 men were confined within its wooden walls. Of these, 730 were transferred to other stations, 3,876 were exchanged, 1,960 died while in confinement, 41 made successful escapes, 5,581 were paroled home, and approximately 4,000 enlisted in Federal units slated for Western duty. According to extant records, 213 civilian prisoners were also kept at Rock Island until the last months of the prison's existence. Of this number, 197 were from Missouri. Their presence caused some trouble for Colonel Johnson because a steady stream of friends and relatives from Missouri poured onto the island. This element soon reached such proportions that Colonel Johnson wrote to General G. M. Dodge, in command at St. Louis, requesting the publication in the Missouri newspapers of regulations concerning visits to prisoner-of-war camps.

Two months after Lee's surrender, Rock Island Barracks still had

20 *Ibid.*, VII, 1284; VIII, 36-39.   21 Prison files, Browning Museum.

1,112 prisoners in confinement; yet during June, 1865, 1,090 were released, eight escaped, and twelve died. By July 11, the prison was empty save for a company of forty men and Colonel Johnson, who remained to close out his records.[22]

The buildings of the prison command, consisting of 214 wood structures, along with 116,589 pounds of cast-iron water pipe and 1,400 feet of small wrought-iron pipe, were turned over to the Ordnance Department on August 7, 1865, for the sum of $89,113. This represented one-third of the original cost. Most of the buildings were used as storehouses for captured and surplus ordanance items of the Civil War. A few more were used as barracks, officers' quarters, and a hospital, the last remaining in use until 1909.[23]

Nothing remains of the prison buildings today; visitors to Rock Island see little to recall this tragic period in the island's history. The mansion of the Commanding General of the Ordnance Weapons Command now stands where once the headquarters buildings of the prison were located. The stockade and the prison barracks area is now a part of the Rock Island Arsenal Golf Course and officers' quarters. Two Arsenal shop buildings stand on the site of the non-contagious disease hospital. Likewise have the pest houses given way to machine shops. All that remains to remind one of the role played by Rock Island in the Civil War are the Confederate and National Cemeteries, which lie in serene groves of elms and oaks. Perpetual care of the graves makes these sites, the white headstones in long, straight rows, reverent resting places for those who died so far from home and friends.

[22] *OR*, VIII, 1002.   [23] Prison files, Browning Museum.

A GENERAL BEHIND BARS:
NEAL DOW IN LIBBY PRISON

Edited by Frank L. Byrne

An historian of Civil War prisons sometimes wearily suspects that every inmate of Libby, the Confederate prison for Union officers at Richmond, must have later written an account of his experience. Many of the Libbyans, being highly literate, spent some of their idle hours in keeping diaries and other records of prison life. The prison penmen often used these as the basis of descriptions of Libby, which ranged in tone from bitter invective in the immediate postwar period to a tolerant sentimentality by the turn of the century. Yet, even with a wealth of evidence, the historian of Libby is impoverished by the lack of primary sources undebased by subsequent revision. All too many of the published diaries and the reminiscences based upon them bear traces of their author's clipping and polishing of the historical coin. Hence the publication of a diary unaltered by its keeper may be a worthwhile addition to the already rich treasury of Libbyana.[1]

The identity of the diarist himself, Neal Dow, gives additional significance to his work.[2] A native of Portland, Maine, Dow had won nationwide fame in the 1850's through his authorship of the "Maine Law" against liquor-selling, and through his partially-successful campaign to spread prohibition. In several states he and his followers were important elements in the political fusions which created the Republican party. Dow, who was also an ardent abolitionist, welcomed the Civil War as an opporunity to break the South's political power and free its enslaved Negroes. In the fall of 1861, at the age of fifty-seven, he re-

---

DR. BYRNE *received his Ph.D. degree from the University of Wisconsin, where he studied under this issue's guest editor, Dr. William B. Hesseltine. Author of* Prophet of Prohibition: Neal Dow and His Crusade, *Dr. Byrne is now a member of the history department at Creighton University, Omaha.*

---

[1] For an annotated bibliography which includes the principal published prisoners' narratives of Libby, see William B. Hesseltine, *Civil War Prisons: A Study in War Psychology* (Columbus, Ohio, 1930), pp. 261-77.

[2] Dow's original Libby diary, which fills seventy closely-written pages of a small notebook, is among the Dow Papers in the possession of his granddaughter, Mrs. William C. Eaton of Portland, Maine. She has kindly consented to assist Civil War scholarship through its publication.

ceived a colonel's commission from the Republican governor of Maine. He and the regiment which he raised among his prohibitionist supporters served for a time in the Department of the Gulf. Because of Dow's personal and political differences with his successive commanders, Generals Benjamin F. Butler and Nathaniel P. Banks, he enjoyed only minor assignments. Nevertheless, his political friends in Washington managed to secure his promotion to the rank of brigadier general. Thus, on June 30, 1863, when captured near Port Hudson, Louisiana, Dow became one of the relatively few Union generals to enter Southern captivity.

Dow was part of the even more select group of generals who endured prolonged imprisonment. His captors brought him to the warehouse of Libby & Son at Richmond, Virginia, which they had been using to hold Union officers awaiting exchange. Upon his arrival on July 11, 1863, Dow learned that the regular exchange of officers had recently ceased because of a complicated controversy centering around the Confederates' refusal to release the officers and men of Negro units. Moreover, the Confederates correctly suspected Dow himself of having incited slaves to leave their masters and of encouraging the fugitives to form military organizations. On August 1, Dow's captors transferred him to Mobile, Alabama, for an investigation of these charges but found insufficient evidence upon which to try him. Dow then returned to Richmond and, on October 12, 1863, settled himself for an indefinite period behind the thick brick walls of Libby Prison.

Dow observed Libby during its most crowded and controversial period. By the winter of 1863-64, some 1,000 Federal officers were awaiting the resumption of exchanges in a prison originally hastily improvised as a place of temporary confinement. Living conditions within the three-story warehouse on the bank of the James River sagged under the weight of numbers. The Confederates, who were slow to begin making Libby fit for prolonged inhabitation, were unable to secure and transport the supplies needed for their growing horde of prisoners. For their part, the Libbyans did little to cooperate with one another to alleviate their own discomfort. Instead, laying all the blame for bad conditions upon their keepers, many fed themselves upon a delicious hatred for the Confederate authorities. The Southerners, fearful of the hostile and poorly controlled prisoners, finally blundered into harsh repressive measures. By winter's end, they had convinced Dow that they were deliberately torturing their helpless victims.[3]

The imprisoned general recorded the Libbyans' tribulations in his diary. To the reader, its pages trace like a fever chart the rising, burning

[3] Fur further details, see Frank L. Byrne, "Libby Prisons: A Study in Emotions," *The Journal of Southern History*, XXIV (1958), 430-44.

curve of his hatred for his captors. But Dow's diary provides the historian
with far more than just another evidence of the delirium within Libby.
Its daily entries pin-point events mentioned and reveal chains of causa-
tion obscured in other ex-captives' confused recollections. Dow's nota-
tions on his rations, while often bitter, furnish one of the few sources for
what the prisoners received on any given day. Even Dow's often unhappy comments on the weather are a specific supplement to many
former prisoners' generalizations about Richmond's arctic blasts. In
short, the Dow diary contains many of the hard facts needed to recon-
struct life within Libby Prison.

In preparing Dow's work for publication, the editor has included all
entries relevant to Libby and has clearly indicated the relatively brief
omissions from the manuscript. In the interest of readability, the abbre-
viations used by Dow to save space in his minutely-written diary have
been almost wholly eliminated. In a few cases in which Dow himself
made contemporary corrections of his spelling or use of a word, only
the final form has been given. In substance, however, the diary is as General Dow kept it beginning on December 6, 1863, when he opened a
notebook just received from home and wrote a summary of his earlier
captivity. Three days later, he made his first regular entry.

1863

December 9: .... The Rebel Congress met yesterday.[4]

December 10: .... Mr. [Jefferson] Davis's Message is nothing but a long
lamentation over the wretched affairs of the Confederacy—and a spite-
ful tirade against England—because that power will not aid and abet
the Rebellion.

December 11: Yesterday, wrote General Meredith[5] and the Post Commissary at Fortress Monroe—to the latter for supplies. The weather for
several days, has been pleasant but cool. The officers continue to receive
great numbers of boxes containing supplies. I have received two trunks
from home, containing clothes, coffee, tea, sugar, ham, preserved meats—
preserves, jelly, nuts, stationary, molasses, and so forth. Have received
also a box from the United States Sanitary Commission, containing condensed milk, chocolate, soups, *essence of beef*—essence of coffee—stationary and so forth. And a box from some one unknown, containing six
double blankets. The Rebel papers, the last few days, contain the most
gloomy views of, *"the situation"*, though they profess to believe in final
success.

December 12: Cloudy, looks like rain. Yesterday, two canal boats lay in

---

[4] The omitted words are memoranda of several letters mailed by Dow. Unless
otherwise indicated, subsequent omissions also are of Dow's listings of letters
sent to and received from his family, friends and Northern officials.

[5] Early in Nov., 1863, Brig. Gen. Samuel A. Meredith, the Union agent for the exchange of prisoners, had forwarded supplies from the U.S. government to Dow for
distribution among the prisoners. Hesseltine, *Civil War Prisons,* pp. 102, 119-20.

canal,[6] loaded with our boxes. One of them was discharged. Were offered yesterday *$13 Confederate dollars for $1 in greenbacks!* Demanded $15.

December 13, Sunday: Rain last night. Bright, soft, morning. Southerly wind. Very fine day. . . .

December 14: To day, have information that no more supplies will be allowed to come from our Government or any other quarter—consequently, shall soon be reduced to the prison ration.[7]

December 15: We are not to be allowed to send out after to day for any supplies from the market.[8] A sum of $19,000 Confederate money was sent out for potatoes, flour, sugar and so forth. Potatoes cost us about $30. a bushel, flour $200. a barrel, sugar about $6 a pound.

December 16: Cool last night—and quite cool to day. . . .

December 17: Rainy and dark this morning. The rumor is that we shall be allowed to receive supplies from friends. . . . A little head ache yesterday and to day.

December 18: Cloudy and mild, this morning. . . .

December 19: Very pleasant morning. Some officers—3 or 4 Colonels and Lieutenant Colonels attempted to escape *early* this morning. Some of them, perhaps all, were recaptured. Do not yet know.[9]

December 20, Sunday: Cold, last night. Clear and cold to day.

December 21: Cold, last night. The canal, this morning was frozen over.

December 22: Clear, cool. . . .

December 23: Cool last night and to day. A little head ache—better—nearly gone this afternoon. I see loads of ice going by the prison—about 2½ or 3 inches thick. Clear and cold this afternoon. A large canal boat arrived this afternoon with about 400 private boxes of supplies for officers.

December 24: Cold, last night. Clear and cold this morning. Distributing

[6] The canal lay between the rear of Libby and the James River.

[7] The Confederates cut off supplies sent by the Federal government because of Northern charges that the Southerners had diverted to their own army rations sent for the prisoners. As Dow indicates below, however, they continued for a time to permit their captives to receive packages from individual senders. U.S. War Dept. (comp.), *War of the Rebellion: A Compilation of the Official Records of the Union and Confederate Armies* (Washington, 1880-1901), Ser. I, VI, 973-74. Hereafter cited as *OR;* unless otherwise stated, all references will be to Ser. II.

[8] At the beginning of Dec., 1863, in retaliation for the ill treatment reported by Union prisoners at Richmond, the U.S. War Department had forbidden Confederates in Northern prisons to make outside purchases. The Confederate authorities responded by ending for ten days the Libbyans' privilege of buying in the city market. Then both sides again permitted prisoners to purchase supplementary supplies. *OR,* VI, 625, 701, 706, 719, 774, 1014; Emeric Szabad, "Diary in Libby Prison," *Every Saturday,* V (1868), 426-27.

[9] Col. Abel D. Streight and another officer made this attempt at escape through the bribery of a guard. Recaptured just outside the prison, they were punished by temporary incarceration in a cell in Libby's basement. Alva C. Roach, *The Prisoner of War and How Treated* (Indianapolis, 1865), pp. 91-93.

boxes today. Do not permit boxes, but only *contents* to be brought up.[10]
December 25: Christmas.—Cold, last night. Cloudy and cold to day. No
fuel—the tables and benches are broken up, for cooking! The Confederacy too poor—really have no wood, they say.
December 26: Cold, last night and this morning. Have a little wood,
just brought in. It is said the people are suffering—for want of fuel as well
as of food. The Rebel Congress is engaged in tinkering their currency,
which is beyond the reach of help, if they could but see it. . . .
December 27, Sunday: Cloudy and cold. *A little head ache.* . . .
December 28: Rainy and not very cold last night. Letter to wife (27th)
by chaplain.[11]
December 29: Cloudy, but not very cold, this morning. Last evening
there was a well founded report that exchanges were about to be resumed. In afternoon sunny and pleasant. To day, the exchange matters
are discouraging.
December 30: Mild, pleasant morning. Yesterday, received from Sanitary Commission—2 dozen cans condensed milk, 2 hams—5 cans tomato
sauce—cheese. From *"Supply Association"* of Baltimore 1 dozen pickles
in pints—1 dozen in quarts—1 dozen pepper sauce in pints—1 dozen
bottles of tomato ketchup. . . .
December 31: Rainy and uncomfortable. *Roast beef—beef soup—chocolate*—tomatoes—from Sanitary Commission. Finish *Tom Brown at Ox-
ford*—[12]

1864

January 1: Very rainy last night. This morning cloudy but not cold. Yesterday, completed *six months of my captivity!* Am entirely patient, because exchanges are not at present, for the interest of our country or
cause.
    Milk here $2 a quart—turkeys $18 each for small ones—eggs $4 dozen.
. . . Cans of *chicken* from *Sanitary Commission.* Cold in the afternoon
toward evening. Lights not out until 11 o'clock.[13]
January 2: Very cold last night, and to day. The water shut off from the
whole building. No wood in the kitchen. No breakfast until 10 a.m. No
dinner 'till—4½ p.m. No supper. But with *Sanitary Goods,* we do not suf-

[10] The Confederates imposed this rule and began examining the contents of the
boxes when they discovered that the senders were smuggling U.S. currency and
other contraband to the prisoners. *OR,* VI, 483; VIII, 343; J. W. Chamberlin,
"Scenes in Libby Prison," *Sketches of War History, 1861-1865: Papers Read before
the Ohio Commandery of the Military Order of the Loyal Legion of the United
States, 1886-1888,* II (1888), 348-49.
[11] Dow frequently had chaplains, surgeons, and others who smuggled out uncensored letters. The figure "27th" refers to the letter's date.
[12] Thomas Hughes, the author of this work, was among Dow's favorite novelists.
[13] The guards permitted the prisoners to stay up late for a New Year's celebration.
Szabad, "Diary," pp. 427-28.

fer. To day, I have heard incidents which prove that our soldiers here
have suffered very much from hunger.[14]

January 3, Sunday: Cold, bright morning. I sleep very well these cold
nights, since I received from some unknown friend a box containing 6
double blankets. My bed consists only of the sacks of 5 or 6 bales of
blankets sent to me by Sanitary Commission for distribution. My pillow,
of a sack of saw dust, with a piece of sacking and a little cotton—and
a linen shirt for a pillow case. Over the sacking of the bed I have a dark
colored blanket—then a large white blanket—4 thicknesses—then a narrow blanket, single. Over me, I have 5 good heavy blankets—the top one
grey, made of heavy cloth. I have a table, of a wide piece of rough
board, 20 inches wide and 4 feet long fastened to the brick wall, by a
back board and leather hinges. Here, I read and write. At night, this
table is dropped and my pillow is placed against it. The [Richmond]
Examiner of yesterday charged upon *England*, the guilt and authorship
of the rebellion and the war, all for the abolition of slavery!!

January 4: No so cold last night and this morning. Cloudy. . . . On Saturday night four of our soldiers froze to death on *Belle Isle!* . . . .[15]

January 5: Cloudy, damp; not cold. No ice. . . . . The [Richmond] *Dispatch* of to day, says that 300 of our men at Danville have small pox—
and beside them—"*several wagon loads*" of dead are taken to burial
every day!! It must be *cold* and *hunger.*[16]

January 6: A little snow. The Rebel papers very despondent.

January 7: Cold last night and this morning. Ground white with snow.

January 8: Cold. Snowing—2 or 3 inches of snow on the ground. Uncomfortable. . . . Sun in the afternoon.

January 9: Clear and cold this morning. The Rebel Congress hard at
work in *secret session,* on their currency. *It will not avail. It cannot be
mended.*

[14] Dow referred to the Federal enlisted men confined in a camp on nearby Belle
Isle in the James River. On Nov. 5, 1863, he had visited them to distribute supplies
sent from the North. Because of his strong criticism of conditions on the island and
his ineptitude in handling the assignment, the Confederates had removed him from
the post of distribution agent. However, he continued to collect stories of Southern
mistreatment of the Belle Islanders from Federal officials still permitted to go there.
Neal Dow, *The Reminiscences of Neal Dow* (Portland, Me., 1898), pp. 723-25; *OR,*
VI, 482, 485, 522-23, 526.

[15] According to the Confederate surgeon in charge of Belle Isle prisoners, the most
common causes of illness and death were diarrhea, dysentery, typhoid fever, and
respiratory diseases. In February, 1864, the number of reported cases of sickness
equaled one-fourth the average number of inmates. The Southern surgeon insisted,
however, that this proportion was no greater than the percentage of illness among
Federal troops in the Eastern theater. *Ibid.,* 1087-88.

[16] To relieve the problems of security and supply created by the growing number
of prisoners in the Confederate capital, the Southerners had transferred several
hundred Federal prisoners to Danville, Va. For conditions there, see James I. Robertson, Jr., "Houses of Horror: Danville's Civil War Prisons," *Virginia Magazine of
History and Biography,* LXIX (1961), 329-45.

January 10, Sunday: Cold last night. On the night of the 8th. three of our men *died of cold* on Belle Isle. Last night was very cold, and I expect to hear of more cases of death or frost bites. Yesterday afternoon had a call from General Morgan and his staff. He is a fine looking man, was gentlemanlike every way, and very kind and courteous.[17]

January 11: A very bright, mild morning. Have been reading *Like and Unlike*.[18] Am constantly reading and writing. My time is fully occupied in that way. Slept well last night, as I usually do. . . . Gave a temperance lecture this evening by request. The fifth, since I have been here.

January 12: A little cloudy. The temperature milder.

January 13: Cloudy, mild. The Confederate steamer *Dare* with valuable cargo, captured.[19]

January 14: Foggy morning. Had a slight head ache 11th, 12th and a very little [one] this morning. Gave to Captain Metcalf [a] draft on *Shirley* for $15 had of him to day.[20]

January 15: Cloudy, mild. Captain Metcalf and Captain Gregg went off this morning on flag of truce boat, *parolled.* A member of the Society of Friends called on me yesterday, a pleasant and intelligent man. . . .[21]

January 16: Bright, pleasant morning. Cool. Slept well. A gunboat (Rebel) arrived this morning with a load of private boxes, 300 or 400— *20 tons!*

January 17, Sunday: A bright, pleasant morning. It is said, a very large mail came in same boat with boxes.

January 18: Cloudy: not cold. It is said our boxes are to be *withheld.*[22]

January 19: Cloudy—cool. Slept well. . . . *The Examiner* of to day, says *that 70 tons of supplies to us from the Sanitary Commission have been confiscated!.* . . . Cold, windy, uncomfortable day.

January 20: Clear, cold morning. A flag of truce boat is to go down with mails to day. Slept very well last night. Am entirely accustomed to my hard couch. . . .

January 21: Cloudy and milder . . . . Sun in the afternoon.

January 22: Damp, cloudy, not cold. Slept very well. The only ration

[17] John Hunt Morgan, the noted Confederate cavalry leader, had but recently escaped from a Federal prison.

[18] A novel by Azel Stevens Roe published in New York in 1862.

[19] The *Dare*, a blockade-runner, was beached on the Atlantic Coast and destroyed on Jan. 9, 1864.

[20] George H. Shirley, an old friend of Dow's and an official of the New York Custom House, reimbursed Metcalf after the latter's release, which is noted in the next day's entry. Dow, *Reminiscences*, p. 291.

[21] Dow's Quaker family background was a matter of public knowledge. At the age of eighteen, however, he had broken with the pacifistic Friends because of his belief in resorting to war under certain conditions. *Ibid.*, pp. 101-02.

[22] The Confederate cessation of the delivery of boxes was in retaliation for a similar ban imposed in the Northern prisons. *OR*, VI, 973-75; VIII, 343.

served out, is ½ a small loaf of miserably made corn bread—heavy as lead —of unsifted meal, and ½ gill of rice. The latter not every day. No meat of any kind.[23] A very small piece of soap (miserable) once in a month and a half, and 2 or 3 very wretched tallow candles. These are everything furnished by the Rebels. But for the supplies from our friends, Government and Sanitary Commission, many of us would perish of hunger and cold. Our blankets came from the Sanitary Commission, of which more than 1000 were sent to me. Some unknown friend sent to me a private box containing twelve good blankets. *Rev. Mr. Moore* called to see me yesterday afternoon and presented me a quantity of cake from his wife. . . .[24]

January 23: Clear, bright morning. Cool. The 8th day and no meat! Only bread and water. . . . A member of Congress from the *"Buncombe"* district, North Carolina, called to see me. Very courteous. I showed him our ration—he acknowledged it to be unfit for human food. He is one of a committee to inquire about it.[25]

January 24, Sunday: Bright, pleasant morning. Slept very well. Dreamed of home as I often have done. Our boxes of private supplies are not yet delivered to us. And the Sanitary Commission goods—2 months here— are withheld. . . .[26]

January 25: Bright, mild day. . . . Potatoes [are] $6 to $10 [per bushel in Richmond]—(cost us in prison $30 to $40). . . .

January 26: A very bright, mild morning. Onions, medium size, sprouted and soft, cost us in the prison— *$1 each in Confederate money!* Flour costs us $2 a pound! We had about 2 ounces of poor meat, yesterday and the day before, making 8 days, without any. To day, we have less

[23] Because of the inadequacies of the Confederate administrative and transportation systems, a deterioration of the rations issued to prisoners had begun. In their complaints, Dow and other captives tended to cite the worst and least rations issued as typical—while Southern apologists did the opposite. For examples, see Hesseltine, *Civil War Prisons*, pp. 115-24.

[24] Dow's visitor was the Rev. Thomas V. Moore, pastor of Richmond's First Presbyterian Church and chaplain of the Confederate Congress. See W. Asbury Christian, *Richmond: Her Past and Present* (Richmond, 1912), pp. 171, 179, 186, 187.

[25] The Committee on Quartermaster's and Commissary Departments of the Confederate House of Representatives was investigating charges that the Union prisoners of war were not being adequately fed. In its report on Feb. 13, 1864, while admitting that the prisoners had not received meat on some days, the committee alleged that the captives were as well fed as the local Confederate garrison and had been given substitutes in the absence of meat. *OR*, VI, 950-52.

[26] While the preceding entries indicate that Dow had received some Sanitary Commission goods more recently than two months before, the Confederates did stop delivering boxes from the Commission before they withheld boxes sent by private individuals. According to Union General Benjamin F. Butler, the Confederates resented the Commission's use of such offensive addresses as "To our starving soldiers in Richmond." *Ibid.*, 973.

than 2 ounces of very poor lean meat. Our men at *Belle Isle* are suffering
a slow starvation. About 800 of them have no shelter! And after a cold
night, some of them are found dead. They lie in the trench that surrounds the camp, inside the parapet.

January 27: A bright, mild morning. Am reading Kinglake's *Invasion of
the Crimea.*[27] Very graphically written, a little in the Carlile [sic] style.
How insignificant and contemptible, the causes of the war! The Catholic
bishop preached at 10 a.m. on the *ceremonies* of the Catholic
Church!. . . .

January 28: Bright, mild morning. . . . Have just written to Fred, Mr.
Stackpole, General Meredith, Mr. Hamlin, Vice-President, and Senator
Morrill in relation to my exchange, having had intimations from the
authorities here, that they would receive General Lee for me. . . .[28]

January 29: Bright, mild morning. Colonel Powell and 2 or 3 other
officers left, this morning in flag of truce boat. Exchanged.

January 30: Yesterday, a *little* head ache. This morning a canal boat is
unloading about 200 private boxes, but the last arrival of boxes have not
been yet delivered to us. Cloudy, cold morning. Yesterday and to day,
five officers escaped. Being in citizens or Rebel dresses, *they walked out
boldly, in the day time!!*[29]

Today, no rations were distributed, until 4½ p.m. and then, only a small
piece of the vile corn bread, and about *1 ounce of meat!* I have yet a
supply of canned meats, tomatoes, some string beans canned, coffee, tea,
sugar and condensed milk and hams.

January 31, Sunday: Cloudy, cold morning. Slept well. Several officers
have fever and ague. One has died of small pox. Much of the government clothing sent here has been stolen. Every day, we see Rebel
soldiers and officers with our overcoats and pants. The Sanitary Commission goods are kept back from us, and are plundered, as are also many
of our private boxes and packages. . . .[30]

[27] Alexander William Kinglake, *The Invasion of the Crimea* (Edinburgh, 1863-
87).

[28] Dow wrote to Frederick N. Dow, his oldest son; to Charles A. Stackpole, his
political lieutenant in Maine; to Gen. Samuel A. Meredith, the Union representative
in negotiations for the exchange of prisoners; and to his fellow Maine Republicans,
Senator Lot M. Morrill and Vice-President Hannibal Hamlin. The Confederates were
willing to exchange Dow for Brig. Gen. Fitzhugh Lee, the captured son of Robert
E. Lee. Dow, *Reminiscences*, pp. 235-36, 731-33; Hesseltine, *Civil War Prisons*,
p. 96.

[29] These escapes indicated the Confederates' lack of internal control at this time
in the overcrowded prison. But in less than a week the Southerners had recaptured
all but one of the fugitives. See Margaret W. Peelle (ed.), *Letters from Libby Prison,
Being the Authentic Letters Written . . . by a Gallant Union Officer, Frederick A.
Barlteson, Colonel of the 100th Illinois Volunteers* . . . (New York, 1956), pp. 16-21.

[30] A few weeks earlier, the Confederate authorities at Richmond had conducted
a drive in which they arrested Southern soldiers and storekeepers possessing parts
of the Union uniform. They accused the arrested men of stealing from warehouses

February 1: Cloudy, misty, cold. . . . Order to day, that only one letter a week is to be allowed, and that of *six lines* only![31]

February 2: Cloudy, damp, cold. No fire. . . .

February 3: Cloudy, windy, cold.

February 4: Clear, cold, bright. Received $200 Confederate money at 20 for 1 in gold or equivalent in greenbacks, of *Captain Charlier* to give draft or pay in some other way. To have what I need from week to week at same rate. . . .[32]

February 5: Clear, bright, mild. To day, no rations were issued, except a small quantity of refuse turnips. *One small one* to me, that's all, for 24 hours! In the p.m. about 2 ounces each of meat and small piece of very vile corn bread. *A little head ache!*

February 6: Head, well. Cloudy, mild.

February 7, Sunday: Cloudy, not very cold. Damp. *Short letter to Fred last night, by Colonel Boyd. Letter to wife* and *another to Fred.*[33]

February 8: Clear, not cold. Slept well. An alarm of *Yankees* yesterday and last night. Great running about of the militia and bell ringing. . . .[34] There are 2 lots of boxes here for officers, not yet delivered, and 10 tons more, coming! Can't get them.

February 9: Bright, clear, cool. Slept well. . . .

February 10: Clear. Cold. Many officers escaped last night. *110 in all!!!.* . . .[35]

February 11: Clear and cold. Four of the fugitives are recaptured. . . .

February 12: Clear, cold. Slept well. No meat; in lieu, 3 small turnips!. . .

February 13: Clear, cold. More of the fugitives have been recaptured; about 25 in all, of those who were latest (near morning) in getting away. . . . To day, our ration consists of *nothing* but a *small piece of vile*

or, more commonly, of trading with Union prisoners to obtain the goods. *Daily Richmond Examiner*, Dec. 15, 1863; Jan. 7, 1864.

[31] The occasion for this rule was the Confederates' discovery that the prisoners, including Dow, had been evading the previously inadequate censorship by including in their letters secret messages written in lemon or onion juice. Dow, *Reminiscences*, p. 722; *House Reports*, 40 Cong., 3 Sess., No. 45 (Ser. No. 1391), 1101-02; Frederic F. Cavada, *Libby Life: Experiences of a Prisoner of War in Richmond, Va., 1863-64* (Philadelphia, 1865), pp. 166-67.

[32] Here was one way in which Dow obtained money to buy food in the local market. He also noted the address of one of this New York captain's relatives to whom repayment could be made.

[33] This reference to letters, typical of others omitted below, indicated that Dow still smuggled out mail in spite of the Confederate limitation of letters.

[34] The report of a Union raid was false. J. B. Jones, *A Rebel War Clerk's Diary at the Confederate States Capital*, edited by Howard Swigget (New York, 1935), II, 144-45.

[35] Dow referred to the famous Libby Tunnel Escape, which he described in more detail below. While he aided the tunnel-diggers by giving them a long rope, taken from the bales of United States government blankets which he had distributed, he felt too old and infirm to go along. Samuel P. Bates, *Martial Deeds of Pennsylvania* (Philadelphia, 1876), pp. 1058-80; Dow, *Reminiscences*, pp. 726-28.

corn bread! If it were really good, it would be only sufficient in quantity, to be eaten at *one meal* with meat and potatoes!

February 14, Sunday: Cloudy, not cold. The officers, recaptured, are confined in dark underground cells, and fed only on corn bread and water—the cells so densely crowded that there is not room on the floor to lie down. The cells are also foul. . . .[36]

February 15: Cloudy, not cold. . . . To day, our *ration* is only corn bread and water. Our private supplies not yet exhausted.

February 16: Cloudy, damp, cold. Earth white with snow ½ an inch deep. Am reading *Blackstone* and *Thucydides*. The Rebs. are issuing *parts* of boxes to day, i.e. what they call the *perishable* articles, keeping back coffee, tea, sugar, clothing. The prices of food of all sorts in the market have increased within a week, very much. The currency is constantly depreciating. Many of our boxes are plundered of part, and some of them, of all their contents. The prison officials are extremely insulting in their conduct toward the prisoners. *No meat to day.*

February 17: Clear and very cold. Last night, *very* cold. Every hour of the night a guard (six in number) passed through all the building. The escaped officers passed through a tunnel dug [from the cellar for] about 60 feet from the east end of the building, under and across a street into a shed, where tobacco is stored. From this shed to a yard and into the street, the passage was easy. They came out very near a sentinel, who supposed them to be rebel soldiers, who had been stealing the contents of the "Yankee boxes", stored in an adjoining building! The room I am in is the only one fitted with glass to the windows. The others, to day are covered with ice! The cold wind sweeping through. Several officers have no blankets! The act of the Rebel Congress relating to the currency is a virtual repudiation of the whole indebtedness.[37]

February 18: Clear, very cold, as it was also last night. Our poor soldiers on Belle Isle, about 800 of whom have *no shelter!* must have suffered. About 400 went off from here, early this a.m. to Americus, Georgia, where it is much warmer.[38] No meat yesterday, but instead ½ of a medium, flat turnip! Sent a long letter yesterday, to Ex-Governor [Albert G.] Brown—of Mississippi—now a Senator in the Rebel Congress—on the

---

[36] Forty-eight of the escapees were recaptured. Hesseltine, *Civil War Prisons*, p. 131. The cells were in the cellar of Libby. See the diagram facing page 153 in James M. Wells, *"With Touch of Elbow" or Death before Dishonor, A Thrilling Narrative of Adventure on Land and Sea* (Philadelphia, 1909).

[37] The law which took effect on this date required that old money be exchanged for bonds or for new money at a reduced value. E. Merton Coulter, *The Confederate States of America, 1861-1865* (Baton Rouge, 1950), pp. 160-61. Dow's peacetime activities as a bank director and capitalist help explain his great interest in financial matters.

[38] Ironically enough, these Union enlisted men, whom Dow thought were going to a more comfortable place, were to be the first of the unhappy inmates of the new Confederate prison at Andersonville.

treatment of Confederate prisoners by the United States Government and our own condition and treatment here. The effect of the new [Confederate] law on the currency, must be a further depreciation of it. It is now at about 4 to 4½ per cent for gold!. . . . A very little meat to day, *about 1½ ounces*. General Scammon arrived to day—with 2 of his staff.[39]
February 19: Clear, cold. No meat to day, nor for many days, except yesterday, when we had less than 2 ounces. To day we had ½ gill of rice and the corn bread. Some have the meal, in preference; I do. In the afternoon not so cold. A few boxes delivered *in part*, to day. All that's really valuable, detained. A great number of the boxes have been broken open and rifled. All the silk pocket handkerchiefs are at once stolen by those who open the boxes, and much of the clothing.
February 20: Clear, bright, not so cold. A little head ache last night. vomited spontaneously and was better. Have become intimate with General Graham.[40] It is *two years* on the 18th. that I passed through Portland with my regiment, the 13th. Maine—for Ship Island [Mississippi] and took leave of my family on the 20th, at Boston, when I embarked on board the steamer Mississippi with four companies—Lieutenant-Colonel [Henry] Rust and six companies going by way of New York to embark in the *Fulton* steamer.
February 21, Sunday: Bright, clear, not so cold. The Rev. Mr. Moore, D.D., called yesterday. A *little* head ache yet. . . .
February 22: Clear, bright—not so cold. Head ache gone. The Rev. Dr. Moore called on Saturday. Not well, is going to Georgia this week. Sent some chocolate to his wife. . . . There have been issued to us yesterday and to day, *instead of meat*, about 1 gill, each, of a very small bean, called " cow pea" in the south. They are very poor at best, but these are *old and full of worms—worthless*. Another canal boat load of *boxes* (10 tons) came to day for us—being *the 4th lot*, not delivered to us! Our boxes are plundered freely and we have relinquished all expectation of receiving them. We have no doubt that our authorities are made to believe that these boxes are delivered, else, no more would be sent. All these boxes contain clothing, more or less: this is understood to be appropriated by officials here.
February 23: Clear, bright morning, not very cold. Some officers obtain their boxes, by bribing the officials, as I am told. But very few get them at all, not one in fifty. We have a ration of meat to day, about 3 ounces—

[39] Brig. Gen. Eliakim P. Scammon had been captured on Feb. 3, 1864. For a sketch of his life, see James Grant Wilson and John Fiske (eds.), *Appleton's Cyclopedia of American Biography* (New York, 1888), V, 413.
[40] Dow's preoccupation with hopes of winning a special exchange may possibly explain why he writes here, instead of the name of the recently-arrived Scammon, that of Brig. Gen. Charles K. Graham. During Dow's first stay at Libby in July, 1863, he might have met Graham, who had been captured at Gettysburg. On Sept. 22, 1863, while Dow was at Mobile, Graham had received a special exchange.

the first for 7 days. *Letter to Major Mulford in a Testament! Received
from Mr. Shirley a box of stationery, viz 4 quires quarto post—3 quires
note—ditto thin note—5 bunches* envelopes—box of pens—rubber, blot-
ting paper, pins—tape, pencils, pen holders.[41] A fortnight since, received
from Sanitary Commission, 4 quires quarto post and 4 packages envelopes. The issue of boxes, *really* commenced this afternoon I believe,
though many of them have been plundered, in part or in whole.

February 24: Clear, mild morning. Yesterday, an officer sent out $10 to
buy a pair of *drawers.* When they came, they were stamped "*Sanitary
Commission*"! We have long believed that the *flour, beans, hams,* and
other provisions sold to us, were goods sent to us by the *Sanitary Commission* and this confirms our suspicions. . . .

February 25: Clear, mild, The Bishop of Charleston preached to day, on
the Catholic doctrine of *Purgatory.* Had *meat* yesterday and to day—2
ounces. . . .

February 26: Clear, fresh morning. The delivery of our boxes went on
yesterday, but many of them were badly plundered, some of them of
almost everything. One had been robbed of all its *hams,* 5 in number,
coffee, sugar, butter, tea: nothing of much value was left. Some of them
are entirely empty. *The Rebs. sell to us the Sanitary Commission Stores—
sent to me for use of prisoners! To day, a bale of pillows came "for distribution among the officers"—the Rebs. appropriated them to their own
use!* My government has proposed to exchange *General Lee* for me—and
I hope to get away on such an arrangement. He was captured at a private house, sick, as I was, at a private house, wounded. Three surgeons
went off to day, by the boat. . . .

February 27: Clear, bright, mild. In the morning [we] were all driven
down into the kitchen—*full of smoke*—kept there 3 or 4 hours until our
baggage was searched! General Graham and I were called up, and we
came to my quarters.[42] Many things were stolen by the searchers—
candles from Captain Atwood, beautiful specimens of bone work from
many officers who had made them. A great many of the officers had
nothing to eat until 2, 3 or 4 in the afternoon!! Everything done here, is
calculated, and we believe, *intended* to annoy us and make us suffer.
Many boxes were distributed to day. They were all broken open in the
absence of the owners—and robbed of many things—the bread, cake—
tea, coffee, sugar, salt, butter were broken up and in some cases, as I
saw, were mixed promiscuously together. The whole thing was shame-

[41] John Mulford was the officer in charge of the Union flag-of-truce boat. Hesseltine, *Civil War Prisons,* pp. 102, 211.

[42] Dow once again writes "Graham" for "Scammon." The Confederate search
was for any tools which might be used in another attempt at escape. Cavada,
Libby Life, pp. 189-92; Bernhard Domschcke, *Zwanzig Monate in Kriegs-Gefangen-
schaft* (Milwaukee, 1865), pp. 89-91.

ful—and the Rebels will surely find that such treatment *will not pay!* I am told that I have a box here; hope so![43]

Another large lot of boxes arrived to day. The Rebs. do not deliver them as fast as they arrive! *There are nearly or quite 1000 boxes here now!*

February 28, Sunday: Sun a little obscured—hazy—not cold. No meat to day, *instead*—we have *4 small frosted potatoes! Major Thomas P. Turner, Commandant of Libby's Prison, is from Port Conway, near the "Hop Yard" on the Rappahannock. His father's house is his home, "Carry Turner"—a large stone house, a verandah all around it.*[44] Every day, I hear more and more of the robberies of our boxes—clothing and the most valuable contents are stolen. . . .

February 29: Rainy-mild. We have had very little rain in February. Have just finished *Thucydides* and am reading *Blackstone.* . . . No meat—*but 4 little potatoes instead!* Written complaint of officers to day about the treatment of our home supplies. Letter to Vice-President Hamlin for exchange of General Scammon and Colonel di Cesnola.[45]

March 1: Cloudy, cold, rainy. The first day of Spring. Eight months of captivity!! The windows are now all barred with iron, and have been so several weeks. This morning an order from Major Turner was read that no clothes must be hung out to dry or air, under penalty of confiscation, and no one *must go to a window,* under *penalty of being shot.*[46] And this in rooms where each person has a space *only 6 feet long by 4 feet wide!!!* Rations of the "cow pea" continue to be served out occasionally—as to day—instead of meat. At best, they are a very poor article of food—but like all the others that have been issued, they *are old—and full of worms.* In any market, they would be a refuse article, worth nothing. No potatoes to day. We have had no potatoes, served as rations, except "refuse"—

[43] Because some prisoners had had greenbacks smuggled to them in tins of food, the Confederate searchers broke open even sealed containers. To discourage smuggling, the prison authorities also ordered the confiscation of the entire contents of boxes found to contain contraband. *OR,* VI, 483, 1038; VIII, 343; Christian M. Prutsman, *A Soldier's Experience in Southern Prisons* . . . (New York, 1901), pp. 24-25; Chamberlin, "Scenes," pp. 348-49.

[44] As Dow grew angrier with his guards and more hopeful of release, he began to make such notes to guide future retaliation. At the very back of his notebook, for example, he listed witnesses to Confederate misdeeds.

[45] Col. Louis Palma di Cesnola was one of a number of Libbyans of European origin. A Sardinian officer during the Crimean War, he journeyed to America just before the Civil War and became commander of the 4th New York Cavalry. See Louis Palma di Cesnola, "Ten Months in Libby Prison" *The Sanitary Commission Bulletin,* III (1865), 1043.

[46] The Confederates were attempting to prevent the prisoners from signaling to Union sympathizers in Richmond, as Dow later claimed they had been doing. This and the subsequently noted mining of Libby resulted from Confederate fears that the prisoners might revolt in support of Union cavalry under Gen. Hugh J. Kilpatrick and Col. Ulric Dahlgren, then raiding near Richmond. *New York Tribune,* Mar. 29, 1864; *OR,* VIII, 344.

those very rarely and never but as substitute for meat. Often we have no substitute—and sometimes refuse turnips. Yesterday, I had a very kind message from my cousins, the Gardners—by a Confederate captain.[47] Was extremely glad to get it. To day, several more cases were reported to me, of the robbery of our boxes—entire contents carried off. The new order about "shooting" has borne its *first fruit!* One of the Rebels put his head out of a window, and the guard shot him, by mistake for one of us! The order only 6 hours old.[48] Lieutenant Parker of the 94th New York has lost the whole of a valuable box, and I have lost the whole of several, stolen away!

March 2: Clear, bright, pleasant. The papers, this morning say that our forces have been within 3 miles of Richmond. There has been a great scare here. No meat to day, except for a part of us. I had 2 ounces yesterday. None to day.

Last night, a hole was dug in the centre of the *middle cellar* of this prison, about 3 feet square 3 feet deep! Some officers think it is for powder, to blow us up! I do not share that opinion. Such an act would do the Rebels and Rebellion no good, but infinite harm. The Rebs. must see it to be so. *This morning, we heard a rumor that the prison officials had put a large quantity of powder in a hole in the middle cellar,* dug last night! *I could not credit it, but this afternoon Colonel Cesnola and others heard Dick Turner say it was so! but that he did not do it!*[49]

The "Financial Act" of the late Rebel Congress has resulted in the further depreciation of the currency, marked by a rapid rise in the prices of all sorts of merchandise. This rise is so great that papers now publish no list of prices! There are two *private stoves* in the kitchen costing $350 each: $20 stoves at the North. My mess and a few others arranged to purchase one to day, for our own use at $700!! The price of gold here is now about *28 to 30 for 1!!* And the Rebel 8 per cent. bonds sell at about 110 to 112, being about 4 cents on the dollar!! The Rebels are to issue *more currency* and *more bonds!* How *can* they carry on the war?

I do not credit the story about the powder under the prison, not that I think the act too atrocious for these men to commit—but that they dare

[47] These relatives, who were inhabitants of Richmond, thought it unwise to attempt to visit their imprisoned cousin. Dow, *Reminiscences*, p. 711.

[48] The Southerner, who was thus shot in a building adjoining Libby, died shortly afterward. William D. Turner, "Some War-Time Recollections: The Story of a Confederate Officer Who Was First One of Those in Charge and Later a Captive in Libby Prison," *American Magazine*, LXX (1910), 622.

[49] "Dick" Turner, who was no relation to Libby Commandant Thomas P. Turner, was the inspector immediately in charge of the prisoners. A Confederate congressional committee later claimed that the prisoners were deliberately given warning of the mine's existence to intimidate them from any attempt to break out to join the Dahlgren Raiders. The committee did not clearly indicate whether the Southerners planned to go beyond intimidation to blowing up the Libbyans, if necessary to prevent their escape. *OR*, VIII, 343-44.

not do it—for they know that if they should blow us up—our armies would utterly destroy the entire south as they march.

March 3: Clear, and not very cold. A good deal of excitement about the city, on account of Gilpatrick's [sic.] raid within a few miles (4 or 5) of the town. There has been some skirmishing. Many persons thought that the *"Yankees would come in"!*

March 4: Pleasant. We think the United States troops have retired. A little head ache last night and this morning. "The distribution of the boxes" goes on to day, very slowly. They are all broken open in *the absence* of the owners—everything is rummaged. Bread, cake and so forth—broken to pieces; *sealed cans of all sorts broken open and punched,* and some of the boxes have been robbed of nearly all their contents. Everything seems to be done with a view and in a way to vex and annoy. At the rate the distribution goes on, the work will occupy 2 months. Already, the cake, bread and many hams are spoiled—Some of the boxes have been here 2 months already, or more.

March 5: Dull, cloudy morning. Last night, the alarm and fire bells rang a long time, on account of the United States forces near the city, as I thought. This raid, which came within five or six miles of Richmond, has alarmed the people very much, and has inflicted much loss and damage on the country. In relation to the preparations to *blow up this prison* and its *occupants,* I have to add that yesterday afternoon Rev. Dr. William A. Smith, President of Randolph Macon College, called on Lieutenant-Colonel Nichols of the 16th Connecticut[50] and among other things, assured him that we were sleeping over a volcano: that the prison is undermined and powder placed beneath it—*"to blow you (us) to atoms"*—that there was no mistake about it, as he had just come from Judge Auld's office!![51] So we are at liberty, and we are authorized to believe the story. A letter to Secretary of War, and General Butler.[52] The Rebels have shut up 3 officers captured in the late raid, in the cells under this prison, in the cellar— *dark, cold damp!* An hour ago, one of our officers, Lieutenant Hammond of Western Virginia, was shot at 4 p.m. and hit in the ear. This was under pretense that he was looking out of a window, but he was not. He was *back to the window* and was shot

[50] Lt. Col. Monroe Nichols of the 18th Conn. Infantry informed Generals Dow and Scammon of Smith's warning. The generals decided not to tell the other prisoners, lest they panic, attempt to break out, and thus cause the guards to explode the mine. For a contemporary memorandum of this episode by Nichols' messmate, see Thomas F. Wildes, *Record of the One Hundred and Sixteenth Regiment Ohio Infantry Volunteers in the War of the Rebellion* (Sandusky, 1884), pp. 291-96.

[51] Robert Ould was the Confederate Agent of Exchange.

[52] The letter to the Sec. of War informed him of the mining of Libby, but expressed confidence that the Confederates would not dare to blow up their captives. Neal Dow and E. P. Scammon to Edwin M. Stanton, Mar. 3 and 5, 1864, in Edwin M. Stanton Papers, Library of Congress. Gen. Benjamin F. Butler was then both the commander at Fort Monroe, Virginia, and a U.S. special agent for exchange.

from behind. The Rebels are mad with rage, and cannot see that they are converting all Federal officers into relentless personal enemies. *I have seen sentinels at the building opposite, looking eagerly up at the windows, in the hope to get a shot at a soldier.*

One soldier fired twice and missed—and afterward we could see him snatching glances upward—to get sight of a soldier! *"Turn about"!* A flag of truce boat is at City Point with 800 men and 62 officers—to exchange for our men and officers. Among the officers is General Lee, offered to this government for me. My hope therefore of "getting out of this" is strong, yet in some way, I may be disappointed, and am prepared for it. Upon the whole, my fears preponderate that the negotiations may fall through. The rumor is that 300 of our men have been killed and wounded this morning at Belle Isle! under pretense that they were endeavoring to escape!![53]

March 6, Sunday: Clear, cool morning. Some of the guards, not all, are longing to shoot some of us! Their orders are to shoot any one who looks out of the window! and some of the guards will do it, if they can see any one near a window. All the windows are barred with iron. This morning some officers were standing near, not *at* a window, when a sentinel drew up his gun quickly, and snapped at them. The cap exploded. He put another cap on and walked away. Yesterday an officer was at a window, looking out through the bars. Major Turner (Thomas P.) the commandant—said to the sentinel near—*"Dont you know your duty?"* *"Yes sir", was the reply—"I think I do."* *"Then why don't you shoot that man!"* The guard replied—*"Here's my gun sir—you can shoot him. I shall do no such work as that!"* I have much hope that I may be off tomorrow; I have heard this morning indirectly, that Captain Sawyer, who is included with me in this special exchange, will go.[54] A rebel friend told him secretly.

March 7: Clear, cool. It turns out that General Lee has not come up— and I do not go. About 40 officers and 600 soldiers are now (1 p.m.) going off.[55] I think General Lee will come by next boat. I have additional proof to day that powder is actually placed in the cellar for the purpose of *"blowing us to atoms"*, if our forces come in here. I now believe the story fully, as I had not before.

March 8: Rainy, not cold. Head ache yesterday afternoon and last night;

[53] No record was found of such an incident.

[54] The Confederates had selected Washington H. Sawyer and another Union captain to be shot in retaliation for the execution of two Confederates by Federal authorities. The Federals had forestalled the retaliation by threatening to shoot in return Gen. Fitzhugh Lee and another Southern officer. The special exchange of Dow and the Union captains for Lee and two other Confederates ended the threats and counterthreats.

[55] This shipment was in response to a short-lived effort by Gen. Butler to bring about the resumption of regular exchanges.

better this morning. The "additional proof" that I have of the Powder Plot is this—Yesterday morning a sentinel, was in our room at roll call and said privately that the story is true, and that he was on guard over the deposit of powder the night before! A guard is kept there all the time. . . .[56] To day, I learned from a carpenter at work in the prison that corn *meal is $16 a peck in the market.* His pay is $8 a day—equal to ½ peck of meal! This marks the total depreciation of the currency. In the after-noon a large quantity of boxes (300 or 400) arrived—brought here by the rebels though they refuse to deliver any! There must be nearly 2000 boxes here, now!

March 9: Foggy, not cold. Slept well. Head ache gone. A few more Rebel officers came up from City Point yesterday afternoon. The [Richmond] *Whig* of this morning says that General Lee is at Fortress Monroe to come up this boat.

A colored boy is in the Libby. John Andrew Eviney, 19 years old, servant of Colonel Devreu, 19th Massachusetts, from Salem, Massachu-setts, 113 Essex Street. . . .There are said to be in Richmond more than fifty colored men, *free,* from the North, servants of officers, some of them two years here! Some doing drudgery in this prison, some driving wagon teams. Some of the men on the Isle, almost idiots from ill usage. . . .

March 10: Cloudy, damp, cold. Some of the papers this morning say that General Lee will come up, next boat, and that General Scammon will be sent back for him! I do not believe it, as General Lee is sent here expressly for me—but I know the Rebs do not wish me to go!

The Rev. Dr. McCabe was here to day and told Major Henry that there *is really* powder under the prison, ready to blow it up at any mo-ment!

March 11: A little rainy. . . . the game at cards, *"Solitaire"!!* The story is that General Scammon is really to go off instead of myself!! The captain (Williams) and an ensign of the Frigate Powhattan are in irons at Co-lumbia, South Carolina.

March 12: Foggy morning. Not cold. To day, the first time in 11 days, a small quantity of meat was issued, but it was almost all spoiled by long keeping. A few persons selected some pieces that they thought they could eat. There are 10 officers—lieutenant-colonel, major, captains, lieu-tenants, 1 assistant surgeon, and 4 negro soldiers confined in a small cell in kitchen. They are constantly in a dense smoke and are fed only on poor corn bread and water. *They are negro soldiers and their officers.*

March 13, Sunday: Clear, mild morning. . . .[57] A boat is up with 31 offi-

[56] Omitted here are several items which Dow copied from the Richmond *Exam-iner* as proof of Confederate mistreatment of captured Dahlgren Raiders.

[57] Omitted here was the address of Colonel Louis P. di Cesnola's wife, to whom Dow promised to deliver a message.

cers and more are coming with soldiers. I think it *settled* that I am to go, but am prepared for a disappointment.

Captain Samuel McKee, Company D, 11th Kentucky Cavalry, captured March 22, 1863, at Sterling, Kentucky. Been in Libby since April 12, 1863. All others officers have been exchanged since—and he was left alone. An educated man and a gentlemen. Abraham Smith, *colored.* Mother is Louisa Smith, Arlington Heights, 3 miles from Georgetown; both are free. Was driving team for government and captured 3 weeks before Christmas—. Has been whipped 249 lashes.

March 14: Clear, bright, mild. I am all packed and ready, but am fully prepared for any disappointment. I have been a captive so long that liberty will be strange to me, at first, as it was to the inmates of the Bastile, when they were turned out into the sunlight and free air by the mob!

To speak to Major Mulford to demand Colonel di Cesnola in exchange.

The Dispatch of this morning says that "among the officers to go off by next boat, is *General Neal Dow of Maine Liquor Law notoriety!"*

At about 9¾ a.m. notified to pack up to start, *immediately!* I had 2 trunks and some officers helped me carry them. The Rebs. would not furnish a team, nor could I hire one. We were detained 4 or 5 hours, in various preliminaries and *in being searched*—when we were started for the boat 1/3 of a mile, where we were detained, standing on the shore 1 hour more. After that, went on board.

At 5 miles and 10 miles below Richmond, 2 bridges (temporary) and 20 miles another. Obstructions at Fort Darling, difficult to pass. Arrived on board the *New York, our boat,* about 7 p.m. No dinner, supper at 9—Head ache.

Slept little, so much noise on deck and head ache.

March 15: Clear, bright. Head not quite well. Started for Fortress Monroe about 11 a.m. Do not feel quite so much joy and exultation at my release as I expected, while I am deeply grateful to God for it. My *exhiliration* is qualified by a sense of *responsibility* and *care* that attacks me, now that I am free.

The imprisonment at Richmond was *close,* severe, and attended by every circumstance of humiliation. Our treatment, in point of food and accomodations, was like that to Negroes—in crowded baracoons, where they are assembled for sale. We experienced nothing from the prison officials but humiliation and contempt. . . .[58]

While writing these bitter words in his diary, Dow was preparing to carry a similar message to all his countrymen. In a widely-reprinted

[58] Dow's diary went on to tell of his journey home and of his subsequent activities.

speech at his native Portland, he charged the Southern "semi-barbar-
ians" with atrocious mistreatment of their prisoners and promised that
the North would "strike a balance with them one of these days." The
elderly officer was transferring to the verbal battlefield his war for the
conquest of his captors. He had not long to wait for victory. In little more
than a year, Libby had become a Union prison for captured Confederates. Dow lived to see the entire building carried off to Chicago in 1889
to become a Northern museum. By then, the spirit of sectional reconcil-
iation had dulled the edge of his wrath. Before his death in 1897, the
former Libbyan even reminisced that he had "suffered few discomforts
that could have been reasonably avoided" by his jailers. Yet he left his
prison diary, its pages embellished with accusing fingers, to point
whence he had come on his personal Road to Reunion.[59]

[59] New York *Tribune*, Mar. 29, 1864; Byrne, "Libby Prison," pp. 442-43; Dow,
Reminiscences, pp. 704, 718.

THE SCOURGE OF ELMIRA

James I. Robertson, Jr.

In the past century embittered veterans, biased writers, and imaginative novelists have poured fourth reams of printed matter emphasizing (and often exaggerating) prison life at Andersonville. Largely forgotten in this never-ending avalanche of persecution is the uncontestable fact that Northern prisons killed more than their share of Southern soldiers. And far at the head of the list was Elmira Prison Camp, whose 24 per cent death rate topped even that of the more publicized compound at Camp Sumter, Georgia.[1]

The more than 150 soldier prisons of the 1860's had little similarity to one another except in the five broad classes into which they loosely fitted. Some, like Fort Warren and Castle Pinckney, were fortifications. Libby and St. Louis's Gratiot Street Prison were simply old buildings converted into compounds. Clusters of tents under heavy guard characterized Point Lookout and Belle Isle, while Andersonville and Salisbury were stockades containing prisoner-made shelters.

Elmira represented the fifth class, that of the enclosed barracks. Although Confederates at this prison were housed in quarters formerly occupied by Federal recruits, their suffering was real and intense. "Talk about Camp Chase, Rock Island, or any other prison as you please," a member of the 1st Alabama Heavy Artillery wrote after the war, "but Elmira was nearer Hades than I thought any place could be made by human cruelty." A Texas soldier stated more succinctly: "If there was ever a hell on earth, Elmira prison was that hell."[2]

Elmira, New York, lies in fertile farm country some five miles from the Pennsylvania line. The secession of the Southern States seemed a remote event to most of Elmira's 15,000 citizens until the summer of 1861, when

DR. ROBERTSON, *retiring editor of* Civil War History, *is now Executive Director of the National Civil War Centennial Commission, Washington, D.C. Among his publications is a recent article on Confederate prisons at Danville, Virginia, his home town.*

[1] The 24 per cent figure is a conservative estimate. Some sources put Elmira's mortality rate as high as 28-32.5 per cent. *The Nation*, L (1890), 87; *Confederate Veteran*, XXXVII (1929), 157; Clay D. Holmes, *Elmira Prison Camp* (New York, 1912), pp. 254-55. Hereafter cited as Holmes, *Elmira*.

[2] *Confederate Veteran*, XX (1912), 327; XXXIV (1926), 379.

the governor approved a plan establishing a rendezvous camp near the city for New York recruits.[3]

The story of Elmira Prison Camp began on May 15, 1864, when Adjutant General E. D. Townsend reported that several barracks at Elmira were unoccupied and could be used for "a large number of those lately captured." Five days later, Elmira's commanding officer, Colonel Seth Eastman, received instructions to "set apart the barracks on the Chemung River at Elmira as a depot" for as many as 10,000 prisoners who would shortly be transferred there from other Northern compounds. Federal officials further ordered Eastman to construct a twelve-foot-high fence, framed on the outside with a sentry's walk four feet below the top, and built at a safe distance from the barracks in order "that prisoners may not approach it unseen." Total cost of the conversion was estimated at $2,000.[4]

Eastman sent an optimistic reply on May 23. Two barracks, "built to comfortably accomodate 3,000 troops without crowding," had been set aside for 4,000 prisoners. An additional 1,000 men could be quartered in tents on surrounding grounds. The camp bakery had adequate facilities for feeding 5,000 prisoners. No camp hospital existed, Eastman apologetically reported, but tents were available for any men who might become ill. Not until two weeks before the first contingent of Confederates arrived did Commissary General of Prisons William Hoffman point out again to Eastman that 10,000 prisoners might ultimately be sent to Elmira. Eastman to the end made preparations to receive only 5,000 men.[5]

On June 30, 1864, Eastman wired Adjutant General Lorenzo Thomas that Elmira Prison Camp was ready for its first occupants.[6] A more unsanitary spot could not have been chosen. The 30-acre site was along and below the banks of the Chemung River. A one-acre lagoon of stagnant water, a backwash from the river, stood within the stockade and would soon give rise to several epidemics. Called Foster's Pond, the pool served as a latrine and garbage dump. The area of the prison, according to a medical director, was "a gravel deposit sloping at two-thirds of its

[3] Of New York recruits who assembled at Elmira, one prisoner observed wryly: "Here they were kept till they graduated in the manual of arms, and squandered their bounty-money, when they were incontinently bundled off to the front, a performance which, according to the most authentic averments, resulted in the absconding of twenty-five per cent of the patriots before they ever came in sight of a camp sample of 'the old flag.'" A. M. Keiley, *In Vinculis; or, The Prisoner of War* (New York, 1866), pp. 128-29. Hereafter cited as Keiley, *In Vinculis.*

[4] U.S. War Dept. (comp.) *War of the Rebellion: A Compilation of the Official Records of the Union and Confederate Armies* (Washington, 1880-1901), Ser. II, II, 152; VII, 146. Hereafter cited as *OR;* all references will be to Ser. II.

[5] *Ibid.*, II, 394; VII, 157.   [6] *Ibid.*, VII, 424-25.

distance from the front toward the river to a stagnant pond of water. . .
between which and the river is high."[7] Prison buildings were located
on the high northern bank of the pond; the lower (southern) level,
known to flood easily, later became a hospital area for hundreds of smallpox and diarrhea victims.

Inside the prison pen stood thirty-five two-story barracks, each of
which measured 100 by 20 feet. Ceilings were barely high enough to
accommodate two rows of crude bunks along the walls. Unsealed roofs
characterized the wooden buildings. The flooring, hastily assembled of
green lumber and lacking foundations, afforded little resistance to either
wind or water.[8] Behind the rows of barracks was a group of buildings
converted into dispensary, adjutant's office and guard rooms. To their
rear, extending to the northern bank of Foster's Pond, were the cook-
houses and mess halls. The first groups of prisoners to arrive at Elmira
quickly crowded the allotted barracks. Subsequent arrivals lived in
"A" tents scattered around the prison area.

At the time of their arrival, most prisoners were unaware of one
last and deadly factor. Elmira, a Virginian contemptuously wrote, was
"in the hyperborean regions of New York, where for at least four months
of every year, any thing short of a polar-bear would find locomotion
impracticable." Another native of the Old Dominion put it more bluntly:
the compound "was a pleasant summer prison for Southern soldiers, but
an excellent place for them to find their graves in the winter."[9]

Early in July, Colonel A. G. Draper, commanding the Point Lookout
pen, received orders to start 2,000 of his prisoners for Elmira. They were
to be divided into groups of 400, with 100 guards for each party. Prisoners and guards all received two days' rations. The Confederates stood
in line for smallpox vaccinations, then marched aboard what a member
of Stuart's Horse Artillery termed "a miserable old Government transport only fitted to carry cattle." The ship's hold, he added, "was sickening in the extreme . . . A large number of the men being already sick
when placed on board, their wretched condition upon the voyage can
be imagined better than described."[10]

From New York the first contingent traveled by train to Elmira. Prisoners were pleasantly surprised when sympathetic citizens at many
stops distributed food and clothing to them. Yet, observed Anthony

[7] Ibid., 1092.
[8] See Holmes, Elmira, p. 18; Marcus B. Toney, The Privations of a Private (Nashville, 1907), p. 93. Hereafter cited as Toney, Privations.
[9] OR, VII, 989-90; Keiley, In Vinculis, pp. 129, 131, 136; John R. King, My Experiences in the Confederate Army and in Northern Prisons (Clarksburg, W. Va.,
1917), p. 33. Hereafter cited as King, Experiences.
[10] OR, VII, 424, "Reminiscences of Walter D. Addison," Thomas Jefferson Green
Papers, Southern Historical Collection, University of North Carolina. Hereafter
cited as Addison, "Reminiscences."

Keiley, a former Virginia politician, "these agreeable incidents were ocassionally diversified by the insults of some sleek non-combatant, whose valiant soul found congenial occupation in fearful threats of our indiscriminate massacre, if he could only lay hands on us."[11]

The first group reached Elmira at 6 a.m. on July 6 and numbered 399 men—one soldier having escaped en route. The second contingent (249 prisoners) arrived early on the morning of July 11, followed by 502 Confederates on the following day. "They were made up of two classes," one observer noted, "the old and the young, middle age having a very small representation. They wore all sorts of nondescript uniforms, beside the dark, dirty gray. Some had nothing on but drawers and shirts." A prison guard described the Confederates as "pale and emaciated, hollow-eyed and dispirited in every act and movement." To make matters worse, the vaccine meted out to the prisoners at Point Lookout was not of superior quality. Noted on many arms "were great sores, big enough, it seemed, to put your fist in."[12]

A calamity which befell the fourth group of prisoners transferred to Elmira gave an omen of evil days ahead. On July 15, an Erie Railroad train jammed with prisoners collided with a freight train near the hamlet of Shohola. Casualties included forty-eight prisoners and seventeen guards killed, 100 prisoners and eighteen guards injured. "With wise foresight," a local newspaper proclaimed, Colonel Eastman dispatched wagons lined with straw to pick up the injured and transport them to the prison. Those not prostrate "were carefully helped by their comrades and others" into wagons for the short ride to Elmira. What the newspaper neglected to state was that, several days after the wreck, Confederate prisoners still lay in makeshift hospitals at Elmira, their wounds unattended and clothing stuck fast to the dried blood of cuts and fractures.[13] On the other hand, a semi-literate Tarheel soldier reassured his wife in his first letter home: "I got heart in comeing up hear by the cars runing together but I am not confined... Wee are fareing very well and are treated very cind, more so than I thought wee would bee."[14]

Yet conditions at Elmira, anything but satisfactory at the outset, worsened rapidly in the ensuing weeks. By the end of July, 4,424 prisoners were packed in the compound, with another 3,000 then en route

[11] Keiley, *In Vinculis*, p. 125.

[12] Allegedly, the first prisoner to enter Elmira was Pvt. A. J. Madra of Tarboro, N.C., who survived the ordeal. *Ibid.*, p. 129; Holmes, *Elmira*, pp. 27-29, 84, 294, 307-08.

[13] Five unharmed prisoners made their escape in the confusion of the wreck. Undated newspaper clipping, Zoe Jane Campbell Papers, Duke University; Keiley, *In Vinculis*, p. 155; Holmes, *Elmira*, pp. 31-33.

[14] Albert G. Smith to his wife, July 25, 1864, Hilder D. Dickens Papers, Duke University.

from Point Lookout. The total number leaped to 9,600 by mid-August and put Colonel Eastman in a quandary. First, he reported to Washington that mess facilities could not cope with so many prisoners, it requiring three hours to feed 10,000 men in shifts of 1,800 at a time. Colonel Hoffman brusquely replied two weeks later that if the prisoners "can get through their breakfast by 11 a.m. and their dinner by 6 p.m., nothing more is necessary."[15]

Of more acute anxiety, however, was Foster's Pond. The continual dumping of garbage and sewage into the slimy pool in the last hot days of summer produced "a condition offensive to the nostrils and dangerous to the health." One of the surgeons at the prison stated the case more pointedly. An average of 7,000 prisoners, he computed, released daily over 2,600 gallons of urine—"highly loaded with nitrogenous material"—into Foster's Pond. Moreover, he added, "the pond received the contents of the sinks and garbage of the camp until it became so offensive that vaults were dug on the banks of the pond for sinks and the whole left a festering mass of corruption, impregnating the entire atmosphere of the camp with its pestilential odors, night and day."[16] Colonel Eastman called Washington's attention to this offensive condition as early as August 17; not until late October, however, did he receive permission to use prisoner labor for constructing drainage ditches to remove the stagnant water and its rotting matter. By December the odor was gone, yet scores of prisoners were then down with disease.[17]

A third problem to beset Eastman at the outset was that of housing. Less than a month after the prison camp opened, almost 10,000 Confederates swarmed inside the stockade walls. Tents ran out on August 7; a new shipment reached Elmira on August 12, but were inadequate in number for the endless stream of men marching from the railroad depot to the stockade. Hundreds of half-clothed prisoners found it necessary to sleep in the open, many of them without blankets. Moreover, a medical inspector late in November pronounced the barracks to be "of green lumber, which is cracking, splitting, and warping in every direction."[18]

Late in September, in a feeble effort to lessen the numbers confined at Elmira, Colonel Hoffman issued a directive from Washington. Colonel Eastman would segregate all physically unfit prisoners for exchange. Hoffman emphasized that no Confederates would be shipped southward

15 OR, VII, 467, 692, 786; VIII, 997.
16 A three-month drought during this period added to the misery and stench. Ibid., VII, 603-04, 1092; Holmes, Elmira, pp. 48, 56-57.
17 Ibid., pp. 54-56, 58; OR, VII, 1003-05, 1025, 1124, 1146. Some 125 prisoners, laboring eight hours a day, succeeded in laying 1,000 feet of wooden pipe from the pond downstream to the river—a distance of 3,000 feet. The War Dept. approved $120 to remove the evil, which led directly to many of the 994 deaths that occurred during this period.
18 OR, VII, 1136. See also ibid., 560, 584, 918-19. Cf. Holmes, Elmira, p. 66.

who were "too feeble to endure the journey." In closing, Hoffman directed Colonel Benjamin F. Tracy, who succeeded Eastman when the latter resigned from service because of poor health, to "have a careful inspection of the prisoners made by medical officers to select those who shall be transferred."

On October 14, five Washington surgeons examined the 1,200 prisoners who arrived by train at the capital. Five Confederates had died en route; scores of others were reported by one doctor as being "unable to bear the journey." The physical condition of many of these men, he added, "was distressing in the extreme, and they should never have been permitted to leave Elmira." Attendants instantly removed those closest to death to Washington hospitals. By the time the train screeched to a halt at the City Point exchange base, forty men were reported dying and another sixty were pronounced "totally unfit for travel." Surgeon C. F. H. Campbell wrote a strong letter to Hoffman: "These men are debilitated from long sickness to such a degree that it was necessary to carry them in the arms of attendants from the cars to the ambulances, and one man died in the act of being thus transferred." The spectacle, he concluded, was "disgraceful to all concerned."

Colonel Hoffman angrily agreed. In a personal letter to Secretary of War Edwin Stanton (who was blamed by Confederates for much of the misery at Elmira), Hoffman observed bitterly: "It appears that both the commanding officer and the medical officers not only failed to be governed by [my] orders, but neglected the ordinary promptings of humanity in the performance of their duties toward sick men, thus showing themselves to be wholly unfit for the positions they occupy, and it is respectfully recommended that they be immediately ordered to some other service."[19]

Despite an outcry that the deed showed "the grossest indifference on the part of the Government" and was carried out in an "inhuman and cruel manner," the officers responsible for the prisoner transfer remained at their duties. The episode became one of the major marks against the prison its occupants had dubbed "Helmira."[20]

In the meantime, life at Elmira had become routine and, in most instances, revolting. Prisoners not packed in the flimsy barracks swarmed around the yards and vied for space within the few ragged tents. Elmira possessed no "dead line," beyond which a prisoner ventured at the risk of his life. Yet Confederates customarily did not approach nearer than twelve feet of the stockade walls. The prisoners were confident that to

[19] *OR*, VII, 891-94; *Confederate Veteran*, XV (1907), 163-64. See also *Southern Historical Society Papers*, I (1876), 294-95. Hereafter cited as *SHSP*.

[20] Addison, "Reminiscences;" Keiley, *In Vinculis*, pp. 191, 194; John N. Opie, *A Rebel Cavalryman with Lee, Stuart, and Jackson* (Chicago, 1899), p. 317. Hereafter cited as Opie, *Rebel Cavalryman*.

cross the imaginary boundary meant fatal consequences.[21] The first troops designated as guards at Elmira were Negroes who, one Georgia soldier sneered, "had been decoyed North and organized into companies and regiments to guard their former masters." Units of the Veteran Reserve Corps and New York state troops later became the provost guard.[22] At night forty-one "locomotive lights," bathed the prison area, while sentries at half-hour intervals broke the dark stillness by announcing that all was well.[23]

Late in July the prisoners underwent a unique indignity. A group of townspeople erected two observation platforms immediately outside the prison walls. For the nominal sum of fifteen cents, spectators could observe the prisoners as they endured life within the compound. One Confederate wondered cynically why "Barnum has not taken the prisoners off the hands of Abe, divided them into companies, and carried them in caravans through the country."[24] A sergeant in the 3rd Alabama added that some prisoners frequently assembled near an observatory to "indulge in numerous ridiculous feats of ground tumbling, ostensibly for the amusement of the spectators, but really in derision of being regarded as curiosities."[25]

For the vast majority of prisoners, however, life at Elmira was humorless; as a matter of fact, it devolved from the outset into a battle for survival. The odds dropped as each passing month brought new oppressions and hardships—and with them a commensurate increase in sickness and death. William Garner, a private in the Stonewall Brigade, was the first prisoner to die at Elmira. He succumbed on July 27, 1864, to questionable "fever."[26] Three months later, during one four-day period, 44 men died, 588 were admitted to the hospital, and 1,021 received "treatment" for various and serious ailments. By the end of 1864, 1,015 prisoners were prostrate, while 1,264 others lay buried in a nearby cemetery.[27] Yet the worst was still to come.

[21] Holmes, *Elmira*, pp. 83-85, 268, 293; Toney, *Privations*, p. 93; King, *Experiences*, p. 39.

[22] "Reminiscences of Tapley H. Stewart," typescript, Emory University. Hereafter cited as Tapley, "Reminiscences." For units assigned as guards at Elmira, see *OR*, VII, 527; Holmes, *Elmira*, p. 44.

[23] "Reminiscences of Berry Benson," Berry Benson Papers, Southern Historical Collection, University of North Carolina. Hereafter cited as Benson, "Reminiscences." See also Toney, *Privations*, p. 93; Frank Wilkeson, *Recollections of a Private Soldier* (New York, 1887), p. 221. Hereafter cited as Wilkeson, *Recollections*.

[24] Keiley, *In Vinculis*, p. 158. See also Toney, *Privations*, p. 106. A member of the 4th U.S. Artillery stated that admission to a platform was only ten cents. In either event, women formed the largest number of spectators, and no time limit to observations existed. Wilkeson, *Recollections*, pp. 227-28.

[25] J. B. Stamp, "Ten Months Experience in Northern Prisons," *Alabama Historical Quarterly*, XVIII (1956), 496. Hereafter cited as Stamp, "Northern Prisons."

[26] In all, forty-three soldiers in Stonewall Jackson's famed "foot cavalry" died at Elmira.

[27] *OR*, VII, 996-97; VIII, 77, 997-1000.

To understand fully the universal suffering, sickness, and high death rate at Elmira requires a detailed examination of all facets of prisoner life.

Initially, one of the more pressing needs among the prisoners was for clothing, since more than one arrived at Elmira in "nothing but my underwear." The cry for clothing brought an instantaneous response from Southern families and friends. Yet Colonel Eastman withheld issuance of the clothing until he could get the permission for distribution from Colonel Hoffman. That permission finally came in mid-August—and then with a restriction: "Only gray, or some shade of gray mixed, can be allowed." This promptly eliminated all but a few coats, shirts and pairs of trousers sent north by wives and mothers; what could not be distributed was accordingly burned.[28]

Winter struck early at Elmira. Prisoners lacking blankets and clad in rags collapsed in droves from exposure. Late in September a camp inspector reported some gray clothing trickling into the compound, yet "great destitution" prevailed. By early December, 1,666 half-naked men "entirely destitute of blankets," stood ankle-deep in snow to answer morning roll call.[29]

In the second week of December, the Federal government issued clothing for 2,000 men to the more than 8,400 Confederates then quartered at Elmira. One of the fortunate prisoners who received an "out-of-date government coat" described it by stating: "For some reason unknown to us, the tails had been cut unevenly, one side being a foot long and others extending only a few inches below the waist line. They helped to keep us warm, but should we have been out in the world in such costumes, one might have mistaken us for scarecrows eloping from the neighboring cornfield."[30] In January, Confederate authorities sent a shipment of cotton northward under a flag of truce. The proceeds from the sale went to purchase clothing for the captured Confederates. All presumably ran according to plan and brought relief to hundreds of men. Yet, as late as March, 1865, a North Carolinian still begged his friends to rush him clothing. "Most aney thing is help to a destatute prisoner," he moaned.[31]

If insufficient clothing, inadequate quarters (prison authorities were

[28] King, *Experiences*, p. 38; Keiley, *In Vinculis*, pp. 167-68; *OR*, VII, 584, 677.

[29] Holmes, *Elmira*, p. 70; *OR*, VII, 878, 1185. See also D. W. Bruin to his sister, Oct. 7, 1864, Anne Bruin Papers, Southern Historical Collection, University of North Carolina. Holmes made the absurd observation that "the sympathy of the officers was earnest and sincere, and their efforts to relieve the situation were urgent and successful." To reinforce his argument, he then accused the prisoners of complaining unduly about their predicament. *Elmira*, pp. 70-71.

[30] *OR*, VII, 1213; King, *Experiences*, p. 38. The unevenness of the coat-tails was probably planned so that prisoners would be easily recognizable.

[31] *OR*, VIII, 23-24, 90, 105-06, 137; J. F. Job to Newton Woody, Mar. 2, 1865, Robert and Newton D. Woody Papers, Duke University.

never able to match available quarters with the flood of incoming prisoners), and the stench of disease-laden Foster's Pond were trying ordeals for the men, other factors taxed human endurance. High on the list of the last-named class were food rations.

No unanimity of opinion existed over the quantity and quality of rations meted out to prisoners. A local newspaper adjudged the bread "as good as can be found in any bakery in the city." Colonel Tracy pronounced the daily soup ration to be "of excellent quality." An Elmira butcher held an army contract to supply thirty head of cattle daily to the prison mess halls, and one source alleged that "all the fresh beef which the citizens of Elmira had to eat during the existence of the prison camp was that rejected by the Government as being unfit for the prisoners to eat."[32] Impressive figures exist in official reports as to the pounds of potatoes, onions, and flour that prisoners daily consumed.

If hunger existed among the Confederates, these sources insisted, it was due to: 1) lack of appetite because of homesickness; 2) slightly inferior quality of food owing to the severe drought of that year; 3) the inactivity and boredom of prison life; 4) the outcries of prisoners whose rations were stolen, sold, or gambled away; and 5) the stomachs in an abnormal condition as a result of long incarceration.[33]

On the other hand, personal records and some reports by prison officials came close to substantiating the assertion of a Northern soldier that "a cat, notwithstanding its proverbial nine lives, wouldn't last five months" inside Elmira.[34]

Many of the first arrivals at the prison camp supplemented rations (which were meager even then) by purchasing fresh vegetables from sutlers who daily visited the stockade. This practice ceased on August 18, when Colonel Hoffman, in retaliation for deprivations suffered by Federal prisoners in the South, ordered prisoner rations restricted to bread and water. The results were foreordained. By late August, an epidemic of scurvy was in full force; on September 11, no less than 1,870 cases had been reported.[35] The prevalence of this dread disease made no salient impression on prison authorities. In October the prisoners received a single small ration of fresh vegetables. Onions and potatoes, wrote a prison doctor, constituted three of every five rations for two weeks of that same month; then their distribution stopped. Not until December was the meager diet of bread and water supplemented with a much-emphasized meat ration. However, stated Captain Bennett

---

[32] Elmira *Advertiser*, Dec. 2, 1864; *OR*, VIII, 65, 77; Holmes, *Elmira*, pp. 89-90, 97.

[33] *OR*, VII, 1173, 1240 Holmes, *Elmira*, pp. 88-89, 93, 348.

[34] *Confederate Veteran*, XV (1907), 58.

[35] Keiley, *In Vinculis*, pp. 167, 172-73; Stamp, "Northern Prisons," p. 494. See also *OR*, VII, 682.

Munger, a prison inspector, the meat was of such inferior quality that a quarter-beef weighing 92 pounds yielded but 45¾ pounds of meat, "carefully taken off the bone."[36]

"I am almost starved to death," a Maryland soldier wrote his wife from Elmira late in December. "I only get two meals a day, breakfast and supper. For breakfast I get one-third of a pound of bread and small piece of meat; for supper the same quantity of bread and not any meat, but a small plate of warm water called soup." Men were dying of starvation at the rate of twenty-five a day, he affirmed.[37] Twice each day prisoners went to mess call in groups (or "wards") of 200-400 men. Years later, Private John King recollected:

We went in a trot, canteens, buckets, tin cans, coffee pots rattling, old rags and strings and long unkept hair, dirt and grey backs, cheek bones projecting for there was little of us except skin and bones. Our legs were spindling and weak. Here we went over the frozen ground and in crossing ditches some poor fellow frequently fell. We were obliged to leave him struggling to gain his position as our time [at the mess hall] was limited.[38]

Hunger caused grown men to do desperate things. "I have seen a mob of hungry 'rebs,' " one Confederate noted, "besiege the bone-cart, and beg from the driver fragments on which the . . . sun had been burning for several days, until the impenetrable nose of a Congo could hardly have endured them." Private King confessed: "I got up many times in my bunk with a bone and after knawing the soft end, sucked at the bone for hours at a time. I wasn't the only one." Prisoners picked up apple peelings trampled in the mud around the barracks, wiped them off on grimy shirt sleeves, and devoured them eagerly.[39]

When rations became insufficient even to ward off starvation, the prisoners turned to a large rat population that inhabited the banks of Foster's Pond. Scores of men lined the banks, waiting for any unsuspecting rodent to venture forth from his hole. If one was sighted, a North Carolina soldier stated, "Such a hurrah and such a chase and such a volley of stones! You would have thought it was our Battalion of Sharpshooters in a charge." One prisoner classified rats as "really very palatable food." A Texan remarked facetiously, "A broiled rat was superb."[40] Once a small dog followed a wood-hauler into the stockade. Half-starved

---

[36] *Ibid.*, 1093, 1185; Keiley, *In Vinculis*, p. 145.

[37] *OR*, VIII, 52-53. See Opie, *Rebel Cavalryman*, p. 319, for similar statements.

[38] King, *Experiences*, p. 36. See also *OR*, VII, 1093.

[39] Keiley, *In Vinculis*, p. 146; King, *Experiences*, p. 45; Stamp, "Northern Prisons," p. 496.

[40] Benson, "Reminiscences"; *Confederate Veteran*, XXXIV (1926), 379; Opie, *Rebel Cavalryman*, pp. 321-22. See also Toney, *Privations*, pp. 100-02. Occasionally, Benson added, rats would tumble into the wells and drown, after which "the water became so unbearable that somebody would have to go down and clean out."

prisoners caught and slaughtered the animal, then hid the carcass in the rafters of their barracks until after dark. They were in the process of devouring their meal when guards (alerted by an "oath taker") arrested the whole group.[41]

Close on the heels of the scurvy epidemic came an even larger outbreak of diarrhea. Moreover, by November, 1864, pneumonia had reached plague proportions. A month later, dreaded smallpox came to Elmira and in its first week struck 140 men and killed ten. Smallpox was ever-present thereafter, prompting a Confederate prisoner to note in February, 1865: "There is not a day that at least twenty men are taken out dead."[42]

Medical treatment of prisoners from the outset was bad, and the continual influx of large numbers of enfeebled and oftentimes ill prisoners was a continually pressing and unforeseen burden on prison authorities. As early as July 11, 1864—five days after the arrival of the first group—Surgeon Inspector C. T. Alexander reported. "I found the sick . . . in no way suitably provided for except as for shelter; diet not suitable; some without bedsacks; blankets scarce." On September 21, ward assistant Anthony Keiley wrote in his diary: "As I went over to the first hospital this morning early, there were eighteen dead bodies lying naked on the bare earth. Eleven more were added to the list by half-past eight o'clock." By November the death toll in the hospitals had reached 775 men. A large portion of mortalities stemmed from nearby Foster's Pond—which one observer described even then as "green with putrescence, filling the air with its messengers of disease and death." At the rate of sickness then present, a doctor indignantly informed Washington, "the entire command will be admitted to the hospital in less than a year and thirty-six per cent [will] die."[43]

If the doctors at Elmira showed genuine concern over the suffering— and this in itself is a debatable point, Hoffman and his colleagues in Washington assumed an almost sadistic apathy toward the prisoners. For example, they ignored or denied repeated requisitions for badly needed medicines. Eastman's urgent application in October for straw on which ill men could be laid received no attention. Eight buildings, their

[41] Addison, "Reminiscences"; Stamp, "Northern Prisons," p. 496; Opie, *Rebel Cavalryman*, p. 322; Holmes, *Elmira*, pp. 318, 335. As punishment, the men were paraded through the prison area clad in "barrel shirts."

[42] OR, VII, 1136; VIII, 39; King, *Experiences*, pp. 36-37; Louis Leon, *Diary of a Tarheel Confederate Prisoner* (Charlotte, 1913), p. 69. Hereafter cited as Leon, *Diary*. Cf. Holmes, *Elmira*, pp. 38, 102-03. Smallpox was the most feared disease in any Civil War prison. For its presence and fatal consequences in one Southern prison, see James I. Robertson, Jr., "Houses of Horror: Danville's Civil War Prisons," *Virginia Magazine of History and Biography*, LXIX (1961), 332-35.

[43] OR, VII, 465-66, 1902-03; *The Nation*, L (1890), 88; Keiley, *In Vinculis*, p. 175; Holmes, *Elmira*, pp. 43, 100.

ceilings only half-completed, were set aside as hospital barracks. When Colonel Tracy sent a routine application to Washington for finishing this necessary construction, Hoffman turned down the request without explanation. An official in the U.S. Sanitary Commission asked permission early in December to visit the wards and to minister to the sick. Tracy, after some hesitation, forwarded the plea to Hoffman, who flatly refused to allow such a visit. By late December, at least seventy men were lying on hospital floors because of a lack of beds and straw; another 200 diseased and dying men lay in the regular prisoner quarters, contaminating their healthier comrades because no room for them existed in the wards.[44]

In many respects, medical service at Elmira was superficial. One Confederate characterized the prison's first doctor, William C. Wey, as "remarkable chiefly for his unaffected simplicity and virgin ignorance of every thing appertaining to medicine." One of Wey's successors, a Dr. Van Ney, allegedly asked the chief surgeon how to relieve the suffering of three particular prisoners and received instructions to give each "four or five drops of Fowler's solution of arsenic." The doctor hastily wrote down "45 drops" and handed the prescription to an orderly, who duly administered the dosage. All three men died of poisoning shortly thereafter. Another affirmed that "for a clear case of inflammation of the bowels, he prescribed a styptic so powerful that it is used to stop hemorrhage!"[45]

Yet the physician most singled out for condemnation was Surgeon-in-Chief E. L. Sanger. This "club-footed little gentleman, with an abnormal head and a snaky look in his eyes," received the censure of both Northern and Southern soldiers for mistreating and neglecting ill Confederates as retaliation for the sufferings of Federal soldiers in Southern prisons. James Huffman of the 10th Virginia insisted to his death that he overheard Sanger boast: "I have killed more Rebs than any soldier at the front." Other prisoners seconded the accusation of sick prisoners "being deliberately murdered by the surgeon." In any event, Sanger abruptly left Elmira in December, 1864.[46]

Throughout Elmira's one-year existence, examination of sick prisoners

[44] Stewart, "Reminiscences"; *OR*, VII, 1093-94, 1134-36, 1157, 1173, 1180, 1195, 1240; VIII, 181; *SHSP*, I (1876) 296-98. Anthony Keiley told of one prisoner receiving a few roasted potatoes from a sympathizing citizen of Elmira. "The poor invalids on the neighboring cots," he added, "crawled from their beds and begged the peelings to satisfy the hunger that was gnawing them." *In Vinculis*, p. 140.

[45] Addison, "Reminiscences"; Keiley, *In Vinculis*, pp. 138, 175. Cf. Holmes, *Elmira*, pp. 45-46.

[46] Keiley, *In Vinculis*, pp. 138, 140-41, 145, 174. Even Holmes conceded that "there was something wrong with Dr. Sanger." Holmes, *Elmira*, pp. 118, 121. See also James Huffman, "Prisoner of War," *The Atlantic Monthly*, CLXIII (1939), 547.

rarely varied. After prisoners formed in line in their respective wards, a doctor and his clerk moved hastily down the row, "examining the tongues of the invalids, very much like an inspector would the arms of a regiment." Blue-mass, a mercury and chalk compound, was the universal prescription for all complaints, whether a malady was the toothache or stomach-ache. Another prisoner voiced the sentiments of most of his comrades with the vitriolic observation of Elmira's doctors: "If they had been dumb brutes instead of human beings, they could not have exhibited greater brutality."[47]

Despite such conscientious prison physicians as Anthony Stoker and F. D. Ritter, the medical profession became one of the more infamous blots on Elmira's reputation. Prisoners died "as sheep with the rot," one of the guards frankly reported. "The number of deaths this week is but 40," a Federal inspector wrote in October with a sense of relief. Almost daily, a wagonload of dead Confederates in pine coffins left the stockade and proceeded to Woodlawn Cemetery, a half-acre of which the Federal government had leased for deceased prisoners. John W. Jones, an escaped slave from Leesburg, Virginia, received forty-dollars per month to transport bodies from the prison to freshly dug graves.[48]

The extant misery at Elmira notwithstanding, escape attempts were few in number. Indeed, the long distance from Southern homes, and the wretched condition of the vast majority of prisoners, confined efforts at freedom to four principal incidents.

On the night of July 31, 1864, a prisoner by the name of A. P. Potts tried to rush one of the guards and scale the stockade wall. He hastily limped back to his barracks when another guard peppered him with buckshot. A month later, guards bagged two prisoners who were tunneling beneath one of the hospital wards and shuttled them off to solitary confinement. The most elaborate and successful attempt occurred in October. Starting inside a tent, a determined group of prisoners dug a sixty-foot tunnel "of astonishing accuracy" underneath the wall to an open field beyond. During the nightly excavations, men stealthily carried dirt in blankets and dumped it noiselessly into Foster's Pond. On the night of October 6, eleven men made their escape. Some went to Canada; others attempted to make the long trek southward.[49]

The most ingenuous single escape from Elmira was that of a Georgia sergeant known to history only as "Buttons." He induced prisoners working in the "dead-house" to put him in a coffin and to tack the top lightly in place. A few hours later, the prison surgeon turned over the day's

[47] Opie, Rebel Cavalryman, pp. 320-21; Addison, "Reminiscences."

[48] OR, VII, 505, 1065; Huffman, "Prisoner of War," p. 547; King, Experiences, p. 40; Holmes, Elmira, p. 295.

[49] OR, VII, 568-69; Keiley, In Vinculis, pp. 162-63, 172, 177; Benson, "Reminiscences"; Stamp, "Northern Prisons," p. 497; Toney, Privations, pp. 94-95.

accumulation of bodies to Sexton Jones for interment in the cemetery. Soon the wagon bumped slowly along the road. His face powdered with flour to give the white appearance of death, "Buttons" gingerly raised the lid of his coffin. Then to the Negro driver seated just in front of him, "Buttons" moaned in a sepulchral voice: "Come to judgment!"

The Negro warily turned his head. One look at the figure rising from the coffin was enough for Jones, who bolted pell-mell through the woods with the shout: "Ghosties! Ghosties!" The Confederate made good his escape; thenceforth, a Federal officer supervised all "preparing of the dead."[50]

At Elmira discipline was strict and punishments were discriminate. The most popular sentence for a rule infraction was the "barrel shirt"— a pork barrel with the ends removed and in which prisoners paraded around the area. Signs that proclaimed: "I am a Liar," "I am a Thief," or "I ate a Dog," usually bedecked the barrel. More severe offenders went to "sweat boxes," which proved particularly trying in the summer months. Such boxes were narrow, upright affairs, wide enough only for one man. Occupants, who stood in an immobile position throughout the length of their sentences, received no ventilation, food, or water.

Bucking and gagging, or hanging by the thumbs, were additional penalties employed at Elmira. An Alabama soldier recalled one prisoner receiving the latter punishment for intoxication. Because the man refused to reveal the source of his whiskey, guards gagged him with a wooden block so wide that it split his mouth in both corners. For his persistent silence, the prisoner then went to the guard house for a two-week period on nothing but bread and water. No matter how severe the punishment, no prisoner received his regular rations while serving a sentence; hence, punished men "nearly starved."[51]

Prisoners accused more than one Federal officer at Elmira of intentional brutality. Two Confederates recalled "the gross indignities and maltreatment" of a certain lieutenant. His "presence in camp was received with terror" because of his penchant for beating prisoners without provocation. A Major Beall, whom an Alabama soldier classified as "the meanest man I ever knew," had a predilection for causing the prisoners discomfort. "Old Peg Leg," one prisoner wrote, "would often visit the camp at midnight in freezing weather, and require the sergeants of the wards to form the men in line, to answer to 'roll call.' " Captain William Peck of the 10th New York Cavalry was "a long-nosed, long-faced, long-jawed, long-bearded, long-bodied, long-legged, endless

[50] *Confederate Veteran*, XXXIV (1926), 380; Stamp, "Northern Prisons," p. 499; Holmes, *Elmira*, pp. 131-32, 305-06. In all, 17 prisoners escaped from Elmira.

[51] Addison, "Reminiscences"; Stamp, "Northern Prisons," p. 495; King, *Experiences*, pp. 36-37, 42; Toney, *Privations*, pp. 99-100; *OR*, VIII, 209. Cf. Holmes, *Elmira*, p. 309.

footed, and long-skirted curiosity" whose chief enjoyment was "in turn-
ing a penny by huckstering the various products of prisoners' skill—an
occupation very profitable to Peck, but generally unsatisfactory, in a
pecuniary way, to the 'rebs.' "

Quite in contrast to these officers was the deep-felt affection of the
Confederates for three prison authorities: Colonel Stephen Moore, Major Henry V. Colt, and Captain Benjamin Munger.[52]

For those inmates of Elmira who weathered the dulling pangs of illness, starvation, exposure, and melancholia, life devolved into a com-
bination of dereliction and despair. Prison officials censored heavily
all incoming and outgoing mail. Letters containing money rarely
reached addressees. No prisoner could have visitors. Occasionally, however, Federal officers brought female companions into the stockade to
view the captives—and in one instance the Confederates enjoyed a laugh
as a result. A pert young lady, in company with Colonel Moore's
"foppish" son, raised her skirts as she walked through a ward and
sneered in revulsion: "Oh, the nasty, dirty, ignorant, beastly Rebels!"
But as she passed one lice-infested prisoner, he casually flicked a couple
of "graybacks" on her. For hours thereafter, the Confederates speculated
gleefully on the subsequent gyrations through which the young lady
undoubtedly went.[53]

To occupy the mind, prisoners attempted many and crude diversions.
Several religious meetings took place during the first weeks of the
prison. Thomas Beecher, brother of the famous abolitionist, was a visiting minister and apparently gained higher esteem among the Confederates than did his kin. With the coming of winter months the services
ceased and never resumed.[54] While many prisoners labored on drain
ditches and buildings for wages of five cents per day, others passed idle
hours in carving rings, bracelets, and other thrinkets which they sold
(through trustworthy guards) to local townspeople. Many wrote count-
less letters home, hoping that at least one of the messages would miracu-
lously reach their loved ones. Some light-hearted souls spent hours in
singing and dancing, while other light-fingered prisoners methodically
robbed their less fortunate comrades of all valuables.

In the end, however, mental paralysis descended over most of Elmira's
population. One soldier wrote home in January, 1865: "In the stillness
of the night, my imagination takes its flight to happier scenes, and the

[52] Stamp, "Northern Prisons," pp. 495, 497; King, *Experiences*, p. 39; *Confederate
Veteran*, XX (1912), 327; Keiley, *In Vinculis*, pp. 133, 172. For praises of Moore,
Colt (a brother of Samuel Colt, inventor of the famous revolver) and Munger, see
Benson, "Reminiscences"; Stewart, "Reminiscences"; Keiley, *In Vinculis*, pp. 131-32,
170, 195; King, *Experiences*, p. 34; Holmes, *Elmira*, pp. 77-81, 159, 280-83, 361.
[53] King, *Experiences*, pp. 37-38, 43-44; Keiley, *In Vinculis*, p. 156.
[54] *Ibid.*, p. 159; Holmes, *Elmira*, pp. 38-40, 320.

contemplation of future happiness brings a temporary forgetfullness of my present condition. I am patient under trial [and] resigned in suffering, for Hope dwells in my heart." On the other hand, a member of the 1st Tennessee expressed horror one day "to see four prisoners in a bunk playing poker, when in a near-by bunk was a dying prisoner." Yet, he philosophized, "such is war: a man's sensibilities are dwarfed."[55]

Frank Wilkeson, a Federal artilleryman stationed at Elmira during the bitter winter of 1864-1865, made the poignant observation:

I have seen groups of battle-worn, homesick Confederates, their thin blankets drawn tight around their shoulders, stand in the lee of a barracks for an hour without speaking to one another. They stood motionless and gazed into one another's haggard faces with despairing eyes. There was no need to talk, as all topics of converastion had long since been exhausted.[56]

Official statistics for the worst six-month period at Elmira tell a grim story:[57]

Month	Number of Prisoners	Number Sick	Number Dead
September	9,480	563	385
October	9,441	640	276
November	8,258	666	207
December	8,401	758	269
January	8,602	1,015	285
February	8,996	1,398	426

The number of sick and dead rose sharply at the end of 1864, when prisoners, trying desperately to combat smallpox, filth, and malnutrition, could not weather the biting cold of a New York winter. The weather was so severe, and clothing so scare, that scores of prisoners stood in snow to answer morning roll calls with only rags wrapped around frozen and swollen feet.[58] Late in December, after repeated pleas to Washington, Colonel Tracy finally secured two small stoves for each barracks, plus a few wood stoves for those men still quartered in tents. Yet even these conveniences were not without drawbacks. Prisoners received small wood rations only at 8 a.m. and 8 p.m.; during the twelve-hour intervals, they had to get warm on their own initiatives. Moreover, with an average of 200 men to a barracks, each stove therefore was the sole means of warmth for 100 men.

"Imagine, if you can," wrote one prisoner in the war's last winter, "with the weather ten to fifteen degrees below zero, 100 men trying to

[55] William Campbell to his sister, Jan. 16, 1865, Campbell Papers; Toney, *Privations*, p. 104. See also Leon, *Diary*, p. 68.
[56] Wilkeson, *Recollections*, p. 226.   [57] *OR*, VIII, 997-1003.
[58] Huffman, "Prisoner of War," p. 548; King, *Experiences*, p. 38; Toney, *Privations*, p. 105.

keep warm by one stove. Each morning the men crawled out of their bunks shivering and half-frozen, when a scuffle and frequently a fight, for a place by the fire occurred. God help the sick or the weak, as they were literally left out in the cold."[59]

Then, on the night of March 16, 1865, Mother Nature seemingly tried to rid the earth of Elmira's presence. Unusually hard rains caused the Chemung River suddenly to overrun its banks. Federals and Confederates alike hastily assembled crude rafts to evacuate prisoners from the smallpox hospital in the flats. Despite considerable bungling brought about by panic, they did succeed in floating most of the sick to safety. Other prisoners crowded on the upper stories of the barracks as the water rose halfway up the first level. Although the flood carried away some 2,700 feet of stockade fence, prisoners had no time to think of escape. Colonel Tracy reported jubilantly that the transfer of prisoners to high ground resulted "with but slightly increased loss of life."

One near fatality in the flood was a North Carolina prisoner who, while scampering from one barracks roof to another, slipped and plunged into the icy water. "I was baptized all by myself," he stated later, "and that is the reason why I am a Baptist still."[60]

A month later, "great rejoicing and ringing bells at Elmira" signaled Lee's surrender at Appomattox. After that, Private King wrote, "we received better treatment from the Yankees and were not guarded so closly." The paroling of Elmira's prisoners began late in May. With the exception of those Confederates still confined in the hospital, the prison camp was vacant on July 5, and ready for demolition a month later. Yet the last prisoner, a Tarheel soldier named Kistler, did not leave the hospital and start home until September 27, 1865.[61]

Elmira Prison Camp had an infamous record unmatched by any other Northern compound and unequalled by few prisons in the Confederacy, whose own citizens suffered horribly from lack of food, medicine, and clothing. The only low percentage to which Elmira could lay claim was in number of escapes; no other prison of its size had so few. In contrast, Elmira led all other Northern prisons in number of deaths for six of its twelve months of existence. It also had the largest sick list of any Federal prison for the last six months of the war.

No prison pen in the North came close to matching Elmira's death rate in March, 1865, when an average of sixteen Confederates died each day. Of a total of 12,123 soldiers imprisoned at Elmira, 2,963 succumbed to sickness, exposure, and associated causes. Of the survivors who stumbled forth from the stockade, an eyewitness made the lugubrious

[59] Opie, Rebel Cavalryman, p. 318. See also King, Experiences, pp. 38-39.

[60] OR, VIII, 24-25, 419-20; Holmes Elmira, pp. 124, 339. As for Tracy's assertion, the March medical report listed the deaths of 491 Confederates.

[61] King, Experiences, p. 48; OR, VIII, 700-91, 714; Holmes, Elmira, p. 275.

observation: "I speak in all reverence when I say that I do not believe
such a spectacle was seen before on earth . . . On they came, a ghastly
tide, with skeleton bones and lustreless eyes, and brains bereft of but
one thought, and hearts purged of but one feeling—the thought of freedom, the love of home."[62]

Today all that remains of Elmira is a well-kept cemetery, whose
solemnity seems to drift with the wind across the spot where Foster's
Pond stood and on to the banks of the Chemung River. The graveyard
seems a fitting memorial.

[62] *OR*, VIII, 997-1003; Holmes, *Elmira*, pp. 254-55; Keiley, *In Vinculis*, pp. 181-
82. See also, *ibid.*, pp. 142-43.

JOHNSON'S ISLAND

Edward T. Downer

In October, 1861, Lieutenant Colonel William Hoffman of the 8th U.S. Infantry was appointed Commissary General of Prisoners in the Department of the Quartermaster General. His first assignment was to establish a new depot for prisoners of war in order to relieve the unsatisfactory and crowded prisons at Fort Warren, Fort Lafayette, Governor's Island, and elsewhere. Quartermaster General M. C. Meigs had suggested the Put-in-Bay Islands in Lake Erie north of Sandusky, Ohio. Hoffman visited the islands but found them unsatisfactory. They lay too close to the Canadian border, they were too remote from the mainland, and the owners of the cleared land were unwilling to give up their vineyards. Instead, Hoffman recommended "an island in Sandusky Bay opposite the city."

The site he proposed was Johnson's Island, three miles north of the city of Sandusky and a half-mile south of the Marblehead Peninsula, which, extending in a westerly direction for a distance of fifteen miles, created the fine Sandusky Bay. The island lay not far out in Lake Erie, but in the protected waters of the bay. It consisted of 300 acres of clay and loam soil, from two to eight feet deep, underneath which was solid limestone. Hoffman recommended it because forty acres of land already cleared would afford an excellent site, the fallen timber would serve as fuel, and the camp could be easily supplied from the mainland by boat in the summer and over the ice in the winter. Moreover, he explained, "the proximity of the city [Sandusky] would prevent any possibility of a rising upon the guard." And, finally, one-half of the island "can be leased for $500 a year with the entire control of the remainder."[1]

To Southern boys who had never seen snow and who found walking on ice a precarious experience, Johnson's Island presented a frigid and forbidding prospect during the winter months. As one remarked, it "was just the place to convert visitors to the theological belief of the Norwe-

---

Mr. Downer *is Registrar Emeritus of Western Reserve University and president of the Cleveland Civil War Round Table. He is recognized as a leading authority on all phases of Ohio's Civil War history.*

[1] U.S. War Dept. (comp.), *War of the Rebellion: A Compilation of the Official Records of the Union and Confederate Armies* (Washington, 1880-1901), Ser. II, III, 54-58. Cited hereafter as *OR*, with all references being to Ser. II.

gians that Hell has torments of cold instead of heat."[2] But to the inhabitants of the cities along the shores of Lake Erie—Toledo, Cleveland, and Sandusky, the weather conditions on the island were little different from those to which they were accustomed, and these temperatures could scarcely be called arctic. Meteorological statistics for nearby Kelley's Island, eight miles north of Johnson's Island, gave the mean temperatures, 1860-64 inclusive, as 32.04 for December, 28.08 for January, and 29.47 for February. The shores and islands in and about Sandusky Bay would be popular summer resort areas for many years. A Confederate prisoner wrote in June, 1862, that "the lake breezes rob the summer sun of its heat, the view of the city, lake and neighboring islands is fine . . . and altogether it is a salubrious pleasant place." Another added: "Where persons are well protected, in substantial homes, suited to the climate, well fed and clothed, it is a healthy locality."[3]

Plans for the prison were approved and the contract let in November, 1861. The work was to be completed by February, 1862, at a cost of no more than $30,000. The prison was located on a cleared area of approximately fifteen acres on the southeast shore of the island. The area was surrounded by a plank stockade fourteen feet in height, with four-inch spaces betwen the upright planks on the bay side. When finally completed, the prisoners' quarters comprised thirteen two-story, barrack-type, frame buildings, each known as a "block," facing each other across a 150-foot street. Each block was 120 feet by 28 feet, designed to accommodate 250 men. Buildings for the garrison were located outside the prison yard.

The buildings were constructed of a single layer of knotty drop lumber nailed to upright beams. Without ceiling or plastering, the warped weatherboards, with cracks in between, offered a thin wall of protection against the bitter winds sweeping across Sandusky Bay. By the winter of 1864-65, however, most of the blocks had been ceiled.[4]

Water was obtained at first from two surface wells, but pipes from the bay were later installed. When the wells became exhausted or when the pipes were frozen, the prisoners carried their water from the bay. Latrines (or "sinks") could be dug only to a depth of five or six feet, for deeper vaults required difficult and expensive blasting through the limestone rock. With no provision for drainage, the shallow vaults quickly filled, and new ones were constantly needed. An inspector re-

[2] Henry Kyd Douglas, *I Rode with Stonewall* (Chapel Hill, 1940), p. 260.
[3] Hewson L. Peake, "Johnson's Island," *Ohio Archaeological and Historical Publications*, XXVI (1917), 472. W. A. Wash, *Camp, Field and Prison Life* (St. Louis, 1870), Appendix. Cited hereafter as Wash, *Prison Life*.
[4] *OR*, VII, 1025-26.

ported that most of the space behind the blocks was filled with abandoned sinks, carelessly covered with dirt.[5]

The first prisoners arrived in April, 1862. For the first two months the depot received prisoners of all types: officers, enlisted men, and civilian political prisoners. In June, however, by direction of the Secretary of War, the commanders of prisoner-of-war posts were instructed to send all officer-prisoners to Sandusky. From that time on, Johnson's Island became virtually an officers' prison, although some forty-fifty civilians and enlisted men could always be found in the stockade. In December, 1863, it was reported that there were at the depot 287 general, field, and staff officers, and 2,274 company officers.[6]

Prominent among the inmates was Major General Isaac Trimble, who had lost a leg in Pickett's charge at Gettysburg. Among other Gettysburg captives were Brigadier General James J. Archer of A. P. Hill's corps, taken on the first day of the battle, and Colonel Henry Kyd Douglas, at times a staff officer under Stonewall Jackson and Jubal Early. Among other well-known prisoners were Colonel Charles H. Olmstead, the defender of Fort Pulaski, and Brigadier General J. W. Frazier, who had been forced to surrender at Cumberland Gap on September 9, 1863. Also confined for brief periods were Brigadier General John Marmaduke from Missouri, M. Jefferson (Jeff) Thompson and some of John Hunt Morgan's officers, seized in the Ohio Raid of 1863. Among the latter was Basil Duke, Morgan's brother-in-law and second in command of the raiders.

Estimates of the total number of officers confined in the forty months during which the prison was in operation vary from 10,000 to 15,000 men. In the first twenty months (May, 1862, to December, 1863, inclusive) 7,371 prisoners were confined at Johnson's Island. The precise number for the subsequent twenty months is not recorded. Yet as this was the most active period in the history of the depot, it can be assumed that the number added during this time was near to that of the previous twenty months. Conservatively, at least 12,000 Confederate officers were unwilling guests at Johnson's Island.

The population varied widely from month to month. In the first months the number of prisoners increased until the cartel agreement on prisoner exchange was adopted, after which it declined to as low as seventy-three in May, 1863. With the collapse of the cartel and the consequent stoppage of exchanges, the number of inmates again began to rise. During the twenty-four months from July, 1863, to June, 1865, the minimum occupancy was 1,710 and the maximum 3,256, with a general monthly average of 2,549.[7]

Four of the buildings, or "blocks", which housed the prisoners were

[5] Ibid., VIII, 330.   [6] Ibid., VI, 759-60.   [7] Ibid., VIII, 980-1002.

divided into small, comfortable and ceiled rooms. The remaining nine buildings were partitioned into two large rooms below and three above, with a small room attached to each for cooking purposes. Arranged along the walls were three tiers of bunks, each bunk accommodating two men. At the end of the room were a number of plank mess tables, each designed for ten men. The single room served as a living room, mess hall, storeroom for clothes and rations, and a sleeping apartment. In September, 1864, two mess halls and a wash house were built on the recommendation of an inspector who described the unsanitary conditions resulting from cooking, eating, storing rations, and washing in the living quarters.

Each room was provided with a wood-burning stove, which one prisoner stated, "kept the room fairly comfortable within a certain range, except in very cold weather."[8] The prisoners all complained of suffering from the cold in the winter, particularly during a bitter January, 1864, when on at least two days the thermometer fell to twenty-five degrees below zero. The wood which was supplied was green and not sufficient to keep fires burning. At this time General Trimble protested in writing to the Commander of the Post that "in my own room we have been many hours without fire."[9]

The only ventilation was by means of windows insufficient in number for the fifty-eighty men packed in each room. In the summer months, the prisoners sought air by cutting small holes in the walls near their heads, to which the Commissary General of Prisoners objected—although he conceded the need "to make openings for ventilation."[10]

Bunks were supplied with straw ticks, and each prisoner was given a blanket if he did not have enough of his own. In 1863, at least, additional blankets were issued upon complaint "so that each bunk for two men has an average of three blankets." In 1864 it was reported that "all have blankets", but early in 1865 the Superintendent of the Prison complained of a "deficiency of blankets." Moreover, in the winter of 1864-65, he reported "half of the prisoners without straw" because the "quartermaster's stores had not come forward sufficiently before navigation was closed by ice."[11] Evidently, it was the policy of the Commissary General of Prisoners to keep the prisoners warm, but there were frequent gaps between policy and performance.

Prisoners were permitted to receive clothes from friends and relatives provided the cloth was gray and the design was not in the nature of a uniform. Moreover, they could purchase clothes from the sutler as long as his store was in operation. Those who had no means of obtaining clothes themselves, or through relatives, were issued extra clothing by

[8] Douglas, *I Rode with Stonewall*, p. 261.   [9] *OR*, VI, 901-02.
[10] Wash, *Prison Life*, pp. 353-55.   [11] *OR*, VI, 759-60; VIII, 4-5.

the quartermaster—but only "if recommended by the medical officers." In the cold of January, 1864, an inspector noted that "few complain seriously of having insufficient clothes, although all need and should be supplied with overcoats."[12] But prisoners later told of insufficient blankets and clothing for men unaccustomed to cold weather, especially those without funds or generous friends and therefore subject to the whims of their captors.

During the period 1862-early 1864, the quantity and quality of the food was satisfactory both to prisoners and to Federal inspectors. In fact, at one time the rations were ordered reduced because they were found to be too ample for men leading sedentary lives. The savings from these withheld issues were applied to the purchase of stoves and to the prison fund, which was used primarily to furnish the men with tobacco, stamps, and stationery. Late in 1863, General William Orme, a prison inspector, wrote that "the supply of food is abundant and of good quality, the bread being good wheat bread." To supplement the monotonous army ration, prisoners were permitted to receive boxes of food from friends and relatives, and to purchase supplies from not only the prison sutler but outside sources as well. One Confederate wrote: "Our men having plenty of money live as well in the way of eating as we ever did." Another man, confined from October, 1863, to February, 1864, gave a similarly good report of fare at Johnson's Island. "The food we received . . . was not, except at times, such as a prisoner had a right to complain of."[13]

In the spring of 1864, however, a radical change took place. Rations were reduced sharply and heavy restrictions were placed on purchases. The sutler's store was removed, along with the liberty of purchasing supplies from mainland firms. Regulations went into effect even limiting the written requests sent to relatives for food. "I remember," one prisoner stated, that the new daily ration "consisted of a loaf of bread and a small piece of fresh meat. Coffee was unknown . . ." He added that as a result of months of hunger his weight dropped from 140 to 100 pounds. The September, 1864, diary of another prisoner contained the following note: "Rats are found to be very good for food, and every night many are captured and slain."[14]

In November, three Southern physicians who were serving as prisoner-surgeons at the depot petitioned the Commander of the Post for an increase in the ration. A statistical check, they pointed out, showed that the

---

12 *Ibid.*, VI, 330, 826-28.

13 *Ibid.*, 661; Douglas, *I Rode with Stonewall*, p. 263; John Dooley, *Confederate Soldier, His War Journal*, edited by Joseph T. Durkin (Georgetown, 1943), pp. 138-39. Cited hereafter as Dooley, *War Journal.*

14 Horace Carpenter, "Plain Living at Johnson's Island," *Century Magazine*, Mar. 1891, p. 715. Cited hereafter as Carpenter, "Plain Living." Dooley, *War Journal*, pp. 138-39.

ration issued to a prisoner was six ounces less than that required under the orders of the Commissary General of Prisoners, and that "instances are not infrequent of repulsive articles being greedily devoured—rats, spoiled meat, bones, bread from the slops, etc." The Post Commander asked for permission to allow prisoners to purchase vegetables, but Washington denied the request, except in cases "when they are necessary as antiscorbutics."[15]

This more rigorous treatment of the Johnson Island prisoners cannot be explained on the grounds of any shortage in the available food supply, inadequate transportation facilities, or lack of funds. The changes coincide in time, however, with the widely-circulated atrocity stories about the ill treatment of Union soldiers in Southern prison camps. Therefore, one finds it easy to believe that these harsh measures were in response to the public clamor for retaliation, or at least as insurance against the coddling of Rebel prisoners. Writing in July, the Commissary General of Prisoners asserted: "It is not expected that anything more will be done to provide for the welfare of Rebel prisoners than is absolutely necessary. . ."[16]

The policing of the prison was a constant problem. Acting Medical Director Charles T. Alexander wrote: "Seeing the camp, you would not know whether to be most astounded at the inefficiency of the officer in charge of the prisoners' camp or disgusted that men calling themselves gentlemen should be willing to live in such filth." Filth appears to have been the condition everywhere. As the barracks rooms served for the storing and cooking of food, as well as for the washing of clothes, everything was greasy and "dirty soap-suds met you on every turn." A nauseating stench permeated the air, rising from overflowing sinks, uncollected garbage around the kitchens, and open drains clogged with slop. The flat country offered little natural drainage, and dirty conditions are referred to in every inspection report.[17]

Prisoners offered the scarcity of water as an excuse for these conditions; prison officials explained them on the grounds that "the prisoners being nearly all officers makes it difficult to obtain the necessary amount of 'dirty work' from them."[18] Trimble protested to the Post Commander that such degrading duties as digging sinks and loading garbage by officers were "contrary to the usages of war among civilized nations," and pointed out that such menial tasks were not inflicted on Federal officer-prisoners in Richmond. One prisoner recalled that even sawing fuel wood was a fatiguing duty, "not that there was much to saw, but that most of us were not used to it."[19]

---

[15] Wash, *Prison Life*, pp. 361-65; *OR*, VII, 1256-57. [16] *OR*, VII, 468.
[17] *Ibid.*, 484-85, 504-06.   [18] *Ibid.*, II, 380.
[19] *Ibid.*, VI, 901; Carpenter, "Plain Living," p. 712.

While these proud Southern officers were reluctant to perform such fatigue duty, they showed remarkable ingenuity in manufacturing articles of all kinds. As an escape from prison ennui, they fashioned rings from gutta-percha and charms from shells picked up along the beach. One prisoner made a violin from material gathered from the woodpile. Each man seems to have built a chair for himself on which he carved his name, the number of his regiment, and the state from which he came. Many of these chairs were not just of the rustic type, but were quite artistic, some having split bottoms made from leather from old boots, cut into strings and neatly interwoven. Their only tool was a jackknife. The smaller articles furnished a cash return to the manufacturer when sold on the outside (with the camp guards serving as middlemen).[20]

For exercise and recreation, the prisoners had the free use of the yard between the barracks buildings. "The prisoners nearly every evening are engaged in a game they call 'base ball' which notwithstanding the heat they prosecute with persevering energy," one man noted. "I don't understand the game but those who play it get very much excited over it."[21] Snowball fights occupied the winter months. In one notable battle, Isaac Trimble commanded one of the sides and Jeff Thompson the other. Unfortunately, the outcome of the engagement is not recorded, although it is known that Thompson was taken prisoner but subsequently exchanged.[22]

Those less athletically inclined passed the monotonous hours by playing cards and chess, reading, and singing. In the summer of 1864, a number worked small gardens. They were permitted to receive any books except geographies, military histories, or military treatises. By pooling their individual collections, they were able to operate a circulating library of from "500 to 800" books, magazines, and novels.[23]

In describing a typical day in his prison life, one prisoner wrote: "Then the newspapers came in, the *Sandusky Register*, a dirty, falsifying sheet, as black with Abolitionism as Erebus; *New York Herald*, and *Cincinnati Enquirer*."[24] From friends they received copies of Southern papers. This privilege caused some concern to the prison authorities, as the prisoners expressed overwhelming preference for this "disloyal" material. There was no limit to the number of letters they could write or receive, but in the interest of censorship the length of the letters was restricted to one page.

Those musically inclined organized a minstrel band which they named the "Rebellonians"; and those with histrionic talent were able

[20] Sandusky *Register*, Jan. 4, 1866.   [21] Dooley, *War Journal*, p. 163.
[22] Wash, *Prison Life*, pp. 194-95.   [23] *Ibid.*, p. 243.
[24] Joe Barbiere, *Scraps from the Prison Table* (Doylestown, Pa., 1863), p. 126. Cited hereafter as Barbiere, *Scraps*.

to join the "Thespians." The latter group staged a performance entitled, "The Battle of Gettysburg" which enjoyed a successful run of three weeks.

Despite the unsanitary conditions of the camp, the health record among the prisoners was reasonably good. The medical services were under the direction of Dr. T. Woodbridge, described as a "man of no mean professional ability" with "a kind and gentle temper," but not well fitted "to force obedience to his orders in the proper conduct of the hospital or in the sanitary management of the camp."[25] Nevertheless, the few comparative figures available indicate that the general health of the Johnson's Island prisoners was considerably better than was that of those in most of the other Union prisoner-of-war posts.

In November, 1863, Johnson's Island lost sixteen men by death out of 2,381; in this same month, Camp Morton at Indianpolis lost forty men out of 2,831. From the date of opening in April, 1862, through December, 1863, Johnson's Island had a death rate of only two per cent (127 of 6,410 prisoners). When contrasted with a comparable 8.4 per cent for the infamous Fort Delaware, or the 4.5 per cent at Point Lookout, this percentage is extremely low. The record for 1864-65 appears to have been even better, with only ninety-four deaths in twenty months.[26]

The total number of deaths during the whole life of the Johnson's Island prison was 221 from among approximately 12,000 men. The Commander of the Post estimated that ninety per cent of the deaths were caused by pneumonia, typhoid fever, camp fever, and dysentery. During 1862-63, twenty-six cases of smallpox resulted in four deaths. In one of his reports, Chief Surgeon Woodbridge called attention to the obvious fact that many of the prisoners arrived at the camp "with their health impaired by previous disease, exposure, and bad diet."[27]

The hospital contained beds for sixty-eight patients; only in the fall of 1863 was it crowded. During the months from September to December of that year, the health conditions were at their worst. The hospital was filled to overflowing and the deaths numbered fifty-nine, which was more than one-fourth of the total for the entire forty months of operation. Except for this period, the sick reports show never more than sixty-two hospital patients in any one month. In January, 1865, at which time the number of prisoners reached the maximum, the number on the sick list was only fifty-seven men.

Even before the prison was completed, William S. Pierson, a Yale graduate and Mayor of Sandusky, was placed in charge. Though not a military man, he was commissioned first a major and then a lieutenant colonel. As soon as it was decided to establish the depot, the Governor

[25] *OR*, VI, 826-28. [26] *Ibid.*, 664; VIII, 48-49.
[27] *Ibid.*, 980-1002; VI, 761.

of Ohio was requested by the Secretary of War to "raise for the service of the United States a select company of volunteers for duty as a guard." Four companies were recruited and organized; and these 400 men, called the "Hoffman Battalion," served as the guard from the spring of 1862 until January, 1864, when six more companies were added. Having reached full regimental strength, the ten companies became the 128th Ohio Volunteer Infantry. The unit remained at Johnson's Island as the principal guard until July 10, 1865, when the prison was virtually closed. During the first two years the "Hoffman Battalion" was led by Lieutenant Colonel Pierson. Upon reaching full regimental size, the unit was placed under the command of Colonel Charles W. Hill, who had seen field service in western Virginia and had been Adjutant General of Ohio.

Although one prisoner wrote that "the officers and guards with rare exception, were civil and considerate," General Trimble complained to the Post Commander that "our officers have been frequently 'fired on' by day and night." Trimble's complaint appears to have been well-founded, for the prison reports mention the wounding by the sentries of a number of prisoners and the killing of at least two.[28] Much of the shooting seems to have been caused by two rules: no visiting between wards after 9 p.m., and all lights be out after 10 p.m. A prisoner told of the shooting and killing of one lieutenant. "Hearing retreat sounded, he started to his room. The sentinel fired and killed him." Another wrote that "on one or two occasions drunken sentinels on post fired into wards through weather boards at candles that had been lighted."[29] One rule which caused the prisoners a good deal of discomfort was a prohibition against more than two men visiting the privies at a time. Another source of irritation was the row of stakes, thirty feet from the stockade, that marked the "deadline", beyond which they were forbidden to take a single step even to avoid the mud.

Johnson's Island was separated from the nearest mainland by a half-mile of water in the summer, solid ice in the winter, and soft ice floes in the spring and fall. Confronted by such a seemingly impassable obstruction, only the boldest dared attempt escape. In his final report, the Commissary General of Prisoners gave twelve as the entire number of escapees from Johnson's Island, which, compared with other Union prisons, was an excellent security record. Fort Delaware, another island prison, reported fifty-two escapes.[30]

Attempted escapes were more frequent during the winter months when the ice was firm and cold guards huddled in their sentry boxes. However, a successful winter escape required luck in scaling the

[28] Douglas, *I Rode with Stonewall*, p. 263; *OR*, VI, 901-02; VII, 1241.
[29] Douglas, *I Rode with Stonewall*, pp. 263-64; Carpenter, "Plain Living," p. 712.
[30] *OR*, VIII, 980-1002.

fourteen-foot stockade unnoticed, the stamina to negotiate a half-mile long trek across the rough ice in the pitchy darkness, and finally, the ability to elude the unfriendly civilians who populated the area. Few places existed in that bleak enemy country where grayclad Rebels could find shelter or guidance. A number of prisoners, dressed in blue uniforms, simply walked out of the big gate with fatigue details or garrison soldiers. Helpful comrades always delayed detection by answering roll call for the absentees.

It was not the fear of escape by individual prisoners, but rather organized revolts among the prisoners (with help from Confederate sympathizers in nearby Canadian ports) that kept the prison authorities in a constant state of alarm. For example, the post had been in operation but a few weeks when, on June 18, 1862, Adjutant General Lorenzo Thomas sent a warning to the Post Commander: "A scheme is reported to be on foot in Canada by Southern sympathizers to release the prisoners on the island. Be on your guard." Major Pierson, the Post Commandant, replied with information that the prisoners had a military organization, were planning to revolt, and "will have abundance of transportation from Canada." In a rationalizing postscript he added: "There was no dissatisfaction with their treatment which creates this disposition, but it is the result of the restless spirit of a set of very bad rebels . . . "A company of Federal soldiers rushed to the island from Camp Chase to meet this emergency, which proved false.

In November, 1863, Lord Lyons, British Ambassador to the United States, notified Washington that a plot was on foot to surprise Johnson's Island, release the prisoners, and proceed with them in an attack on Buffalo. Great excitement swept all along the lower Great Lakes region. General Jacob D. Cox, commanding the Ohio Military District, hastened to Sandusky from his Cincinnati headquarters. He ordered up two batteries of artillery and placed them on Cedar Point, a peninsula from which the guns could command the entrance to Sandusky Bay. Governor David Tod rushed six companies of the 12th Ohio Cavalry (dismounted) to Sandusky, and the Navy Department moved the U.S. Steamer *Michigan* (fourteen guns) to Johnson's Island. Presumably, the plotters were frustrated by this display of military strength; in any event, the rumored attack did not materialize.

The fear of a hostile move from Canada continued for some time afterward. In the following January, five regiments of the Third Division, VI Army Corps, were assigned to duty at Sandusky. With this addition the garrison numbered 2,238 men, which was greater than the number of prisoners confined at the time.[31] The troops not only built fortifications and maintained defenses against outside attacks by both

---

[31] *Ibid.*, IV, 37, 50.

land and water, but also performed picket duty and guarded prisoners.

The long-anticipated attack from Canada erupted at last in September, 1864. On September 19, the Assistant Provost Marshal at Detroit informed Captain John C. Carter, commanding the U.S. Steamer *Michigan*, that "parties will embark today at Malden [on the Canadian side of the Detroit River] on board the *Philo Parsons* . . ." He added an assurance that officers and men of the *Michigan* had been bribed by a man named Cole.[32]

The Provost Marshal's information was to a degree correct. On the morning of September 19 a detail of thirty paroled or escaped Confederate soldiers and sailors, armed with revolvers and bowie knives, took passage on the steamer *Philo Parsons*, which plied the Lake Erie islands. At Kelley's Island they seized the vessel and with it set forth for Middle Bass. Soon they met and took over the *Island Queen*, another passenger boat, which they sank after discharging the passengers (thirty-five of whom were unarmed Ohio militiamen). That night they stood on the deck of the *Philo Parsons* at Middle Bass Island and looked across the water for a rocket signal from the gunboat *Michigan*, which lay a few miles away. At the signal they were to board and capture the *Michigan*.

The rocket was to be set off on orders from one Charles H. Cole, a Confederate agent charged with the job of laying the ground work at Sandusky and Johnson's Island. For weeks he had been living in Sandusky, posing as a Philadelphia banker, although he was actually a paroled officer from Bedford Forrest's cavalry. With lavish entertainments he had won his way into the good graces of the officers at Sandusky and those on the steamer *Michigan*, and so had been a frequent and a welcome visitor both at the prison and on the *Michigan*. The action at Sandusky was to open with a gala dinner to the officers of the *Michigan* aboard the ship. The event was scheduled for the same evening that the attacking party on the *Philo Parsons* would be arriving at nearby Middle Bass. The host was to be Charles Cole; a number of landlubber guests would be his accomplices. With the ship's officers paralyzed from drugged champagne, the signal to the *Parsons* would bring the boarding party and the *Michigan* would be a prize of the Confederate States of America.

On that same evening, members of Ohio copperhead organizations were to arrive by train at Sandusky. They were to seize the arsenal, then arm themselves and the prisoners on Johnson's Island. Attacked by land and water, with a prisoners' revolt from within, the prison guard would be overwhelmed and the prisoners released. A Confederate army made up of Northern copperheads and Rebel officers, assisted by the only

32 *Ibid.*, VII, 842.

armed vessel on the lower Great Lakes, would soon be marching to capture and sack the cities along the shores of Lake Erie.

This fantastic scheme proved to be a miserable fiasco. The conspirators were betrayed into the hands of the U.S. Provost Marshal in Detroit, who sent warnings to the authorities at Sandusky. Cole was arrested at his hotel in the afternoon. There was no dinner on the *Michigan*, and consequently no rocket. Seeing no signal, the men on the *Philo Parsons* suspected that the plot had been discovered. They lost their nerve and compelled John Yates Beall, their leader, to sail back to Canada. Trains arriving at Sandusky were thoroughly searched, but the expected companies of fighting men were nowhere to be found.

Although Cole, on his visits to Johnson's Island, must have tipped off the leaders among the prisoners, no disturbance occurred within the prison walls that evening. The Superintendent of the Prison did not even mention the incident in his weekly report, being much more concerned about a severe windstorm which a few days later unroofed some of the blocks and injured a number of the prisoners.

Reasons existed for these frequent alarms about incursions from Canada. Confederate Commissioners Jacob Thompson and Clement C. Clay were active in organizing Southern sympathizers north of the border. Amply supplied with funds, they were in close alliance with the leaders of secret Ohio disloyal organizations, said to number over 100,000 men. These activities, however, turned out to be only sound and fury, and resulted in nothing. No effective force was ever mobilized in Canada, and the Ohio disloyalists confined their efforts only to sub rosa meetings, drilling, and oath-taking. At no time was the security of Johnson's Island prisoners ever in serious jeopardy.

Much of the wretchedness at Johnson's Island can be traced to shortsighted planning at the outset. In the winter of 1861-62, when the prison was being designed and constructed, a mammoth army assembled at Washington to advance on Richmond and crush the Southern rebellion. Hence, like so much of Civil War planning, the Johnson's Island project was in the nature of an expedient, intended to be temporary and inexpensive. The jerry-built quality of the buildings (void of foundations) clearly indicates that the camp was not intended for any lengthy service. The nearby fallen trees, it was thought, would furnish ample fuel during the brief life of the prison, and the owner of the island would be glad to collect the kitchen scraps to feed his hogs.

Contrary to all expectations, the frail, cheap, and hastily-built structures were forced to stand against the fierce northern Ohio gales of three long winters. A camp planned to accommodate 1,000 prisoners was later to house several times that number. Prisoners who were to be held only for a few weeks pending exchange were compelled to remain for from twelve to sixteen months, and in some cases longer. The small garrison of 400 men grew into a force of 2,200—two regiments in size. With the departure of the last inhabitants in July, 1865, the anticipated short-lived Johnson's Island depot for prisoners of war had had a long and lively existence of forty months.

Prisoners were the helpless victims of laxity in the operation of Johnson's Island. Seldom if ever were all of the camp facilities in full working order. The quarters and grounds were never properly policed, supplies were constantly short, the beef was often rancid, and the fuel wood was green. The water pipes were frequently frozen or out of order, and the sanitation problems were never solved.

William S. Pierson, who commanded the post until supplanted in January, 1864, was a loyal, conscientious officer, yet a man with no military training. With a small staff and a meager working force, he was responsible for the guarding and disciplining of the prisoners, the maintenance of the buildings and grounds, and for all commissary and quartermaster services. Such a demand called for a versatility rare among even experienced field officers.

Brigadier General H. D. Terry of the VI Army Corps, who succeeded Pierson, showed little enthusiasm for his prison assignment. As Lieutenant Colonel John Marsh commented in an inspection report: "General Terry is an intelligent, clever gentleman, but quite as fond of a social glass of whiskey as of attending to the duties of his command." He then added that "little judgment is exercised in the management and discipline of the prison."[33] Colonel Charles W. Hill, who commanded during the busy period of 1864 and early 1865, complained to Washington of his "enormous amount of work." He called attention to his many duties in disciplining and instructing troops and prisoners, and "policing, building, road-making, draining, and repairs."[34]

In an apparent effort to achieve a more efficient operation, the Commissary General of Prisoners in the spring of 1864 ordered the appointment of a Superintendent of the Prison, who was required to submit weekly reports on the condition of the prison and prisoners. If inspections and reports could accomplish perfection, Johnson's Island would have been an ideal institution. It was visited, inspected, and reported on almost continually. Army medical officers wrote detailed accounts of their findings, listed deficiencies and recommended improvements— despite the fact that few of their recommendations resulted in any positive action.

Washington would allow the local authorities very little discretion. This policy of remote control engendered inevitable delays, frustrations and misunderstandings. Authority to move a section of the stockade a

[33] Ibid., 122.   [34] Ibid., 680-81.

few paces, allowing prisoners to purchase potatoes and onions from the sutler, permitting crippled and sick prisoners to eat in their quarters—all such minor matters required Washington's approval. The request of a Sandusky priest to visit the camp to minister to the spiritual needs of Catholic prisoners could be granted only upon a permit from the Commissary General's headquarters in Washington.[35] The occupants of some of the blocks offered to provide the labor and materials for lining the thin walls of their wards with ceiling. While they received the hearty approval of the Commander of the Post, the Commissary General vetoed the proposal on the ground that "to put the requisite tools and lumber in the hands of the prisoners would much facilitate their efforts to escape." He suggested that the cracks between the boards "be closed up with a plaster of clay."[36]

Constantly in the minds of the authorities was the necessity for economy, for they were always fearful of public criticism if any large expenditures were made for the comfort of Confederate prisoners. Even in the initial planning, one of the important considerations for locating the prison on Johnson's Island was the fact that the land could be rented for the mere sum of $500 a year, while the cost of building the project was only a few thousand dollars. Orders issued at a later date by the Commissary General specified that the structures "must be of a temporary and cheap character." In over three years, the only additions and improvements introduced consisted of a slight enlargement of the prison area and lining the walls of some of the blocks, two new mess halls, a wash house, and an extra water pump. Ironically, surrounded by Lake Erie, the water supply was inadequate, a constant source of complaint by the prisoners, and the subject of comment by many inspectors. A reservoir supplying clear water pumped from the bay could have been installed for a meager $7,000. Such a water system would have solved the difficulties of sanitation and would have provided an ample supply of water with which the buildings and their occupants could have been kept clean. But no one seemed to have the courage or the initiative to endorse such a large outlay of funds, even though the project could have been financed from the prison fund.[37]

There was misery aplenty on Johnson's Island, but the prison certainly was far from being the worst of Civil War compounds. The health record was good and, up to the last few months of 1864, the food ration was sufficient and could be supplemented by private purchases. The prisoners, especially those from the Deep South, found their quarters cold. Yet they were as comfortable as members of the garrison, some of whom were housed in tents. The men were given as much freedom as security would permit. They engaged in many recreational activities, were able

35 *Ibid.*, V, 594.   36 *Ibid.*, VII, 1050.   37 *Ibid.*, 468; VIII, 330-31.

to obtain reading material, and to receive letters and newspapers from home. Except in a few cases, they were not ill treated by their captors. On the other hand, being ordered about by Yankee privates must have been humiliating to those proud officers. "Our rolls," wrote one prisoner, "are called by a sergeant of eighteen years of age, who, with an impudent air, orders, 'Fall in, boys, I'm in a hurry,' and this to his seniors in age, rank, position, and everything that constitutes a man, soldier, and gentleman."[38]

Most of the time the physical discomforts of the prisoners were caused primarily by bad management, not design, on the part of the authorities. But their greatest distress was not so much physical as it was mental. The mere fact of being restricted to an isolated island far from civilian life must have been depressing in itself. Moreover, the Southerners were in a harsh, strange climate, far different from that of their beloved and sunny homeland. Their minds were filled with thoughts of home and friends, the dull routine of prison life offering little else to think about. Even good food and a comfortable bed would not have cured the agonies of homesickness—and, underneath, was a deep-seated restlessness nourished by a feeling of frustration in being so useless to the cause in which they believed.

Today Johnson's Island is a lonely but lovely spot with no permanent inhabitants, although efforts are being made to develop it into a summer resort. Time has obliterated all traces of the prison buildings, the stockade, and block houses. The only memory of sad Civil War days is the little cemetery near the northeast point of the island. The cemetery covers an acre of ground, shaded on one side by a beautiful grove of trees. This grassy plot, surrounded by an iron fence, holds the graves of 206 Confederate soldiers and a few enlisted men who died on the island while prisoners of war. Each grave is marked by a headstone of Georgian marble on which is carved the name of the soldier and that of his regiment, except for a few who are unknown. At the entrance, on a marble base, stands the bronze figure of a Confederate private soldier, peering out over the waters of the bay. This statue, unveiled in 1910 and named "The Outlook," is the creation of Sir Moses Ezekial, world famous Richmond sculptor who also designed the well-known figure of Stonewall Jackson on the campus of the Virginia Military Institute in Lexington, Virginia.

After the war the cemetery was greatly neglected, except when it was cleaned up for Memorial Day exercises which for years were conducted by the Sandusky McMeans Post of the G.A.R. In 1889 a party of editors and public officials from Georgia visited the island. They found the

[38] Barbiere, *Scraps*, p. 80.

wooden grave markers rotting away with the names rapidly being effaced. By private subscription they obtained the funds out of which they had the present marble headstones carved and placed on the graves.[39] The cemetery is now the property of the United States Government and is maintained by the Department of the Interior.

[39] Sandusky *Register*, May 12, 1890.

CAHABA TO CHARLESTON: THE PRISON ODYSSEY OF LT. EDMUND E. RYAN

William M. Armstrong

Although contemporary accounts of life in Civil War prisons are fairly plentiful, some of them occasionally accentuate the colorful or the sensational at the expense of the truthful. In a different category is the prison diary of Edmund E. Ryan, a Pennsylvanian who was captured on two separate occasions during the war and suffered eight months of imprisonment in more than a half-dozen Confederate prison camps. Throughout most of his wanderings as a captive, he kept a journal that in the main shows an acuity and detachment not always found in Civil War diaries published for the generation of the 1860's.

Ryan, a twenty-seven year old law-book salesman from Philadelphia, was living temporarily in Peoria, Illinois when in 1861 he volunteered for service with the 17th Illinois Infantry Regiment. At Camp Mather, Peoria, he was mustered in on May 25 as corporal of Company A and sent with his regiment for training to Camp Butler, in Lincoln's home town of Springfield.

The following autumn found Ryan at the scene of action in Missouri. The Company A morning report for October 20, 1861, contained this single-line entry: "Sergt. E. E. Ryan captured by Jeff Thompson while carrying a dispatch to the Ironton forces." The record is mute (Ryan did not then keep a diary) for the next thirty days, but the morning report for November 18 noted that he had been exchanged and returned to duty. He was shortly promoted to second lieutenant.[1]

In the months that followed, Ryan was named company commander and saw action at Ft. Donelson, Shiloh, and Vicksburg. Again promoted

DR. ARMSTRONG *is associate professor of history at Alma College in Michigan. The author of* E. L. Godkin and American Foreign Policy, 1865-1900, *his field of specialization includes the post-Civil War period.*

[1] Much of the above information is contained in the morning reports, muster rolls, and descriptive book of Co. A, 17th Illinois, currently, with Ryan's diary, in the possession of the Peoria Historical Society. For additional aid, the writer is indebted to Ryan's grandson, E. C. Ryan of Winnipeg, Manitoba, and to Haskell Armstrong of Peoria.

(April, 1862), he served for a time as Provost Marshal to Major General McClernand's army. On February 1, 1864, he was detailed regimental quartermaster and ordered to accompany two corps under General Sherman on a grain raid from Vicksburg across the state of Mississippi. For twelve days the army pushed relentlessly eastward, burning stores and destroying railroad tracks as it went. On February 15, while leading a foraging party near Meridian, Ryan and six of his party were seized by the Confederates. Describing the event later, he indulged in a rare (and under the circumstances scarcely justifiable) outburst against his captors: "We were captured by a party of *low*-lived thieves and robbers who stripped us of our money and everything else of value that we had with us."[2]

After processing the prisoners, their captors marched them eastward toward the Confederate prison at Cahaba, Alabama, roughly six days and 125 miles distant. Ryan had now begun to keep a diary, a narrative which portrayed him as a keenly interested observer of the terrain and somewhat indifferent to the conditions of his captivity. From Meridian to the Timbigbee River he found that "the public roads are good, and water quite plenty," but he made no mention of his captors. Most of the small towns through which they passed were deserted, but Ryan noticed that the country was "much better than any I passed through in coming from Vicksburg to Meridian." On February 19 the party reached the "small but pretty town" of Demopolis in Western Alabama. Here he met Nathan Bradley of Marengo, "a very kind gentleman" who gave him $100 in Confederate currency. Still, there was no hint of the treatment he was getting from his captors.

The afternoon of February 20 found the party in Selma, Alabama, "quite a nice little city," in Ryan's description, with a "large arsenal and armory." From this point onward his attention to his diary resolved itself into clusters of days, instead of individual daily entries. As a result, the reader cannot always discern the exact date of an occurrence. But apparently on February 21, he arrived at Cahaba, "nicely situated," as he described it, "on the west bank of the Alabama ten miles south of Selma." Marched at once to the military prison, he accepted what greeted his eyes with what might be termed stoic aversion. He wrote:

The military prison at this place is nothing more than an old cotton warehouse which is used as a halfway resting place for all poor, unfortunate officers and soldiers who may fall into the rebel hands in the Department of the West. There are in confinement here at the present time eight Union officers and about 300 men. Our ration consists of one qt. of meal and one fourth of one lb. of meat per day. Sometimes we receive a few cow peas which

[2] Ryan diary, undated opening entry. Unless otherwise noted, all subsequent quotations will be from the diary.

are not fit for man to eat. We spend our time in cooking, sleeping, reading, playing cards, singing songs, and discussing the various subjects of the day. It is a hard, disagreeable life for a human being to live. Our prison is so unclean that it is impossible for us to keep clear of vermin. The officers and soldiers treat us as officers and true soldiers should treat prisoners of war. The hospital accommodations at this prison are quite good for the place.

In his account Ryan omitted to say that the cotton shed (which in turn was surrounded by a stockade) was only partly roofed. This prison enjoyed a poor record for policing and cleanliness; its water supply was at one time polluted. This was due in part to the fact that Cahaba was intended only as a temporary place of confinement, although in October, 1864, more than 2,000 Union soldiers were held there.

The ensuing months proved disagreeable ones for the lieutenant. March and April were cold, with officers and men alike "suffering from want of clothing." Yet he refrained from criticizing his captors. "Time passes slowly," he commented in April, "with anyone who is unfortunate enough to be confined in prison. Sometimes we hear from our army through captured Federal soldiers. I find it almost impossible to confine myself to any particular study." When May arrived, Ryan was effusive in his gratitude: "Long looked for Spring has come at last in all her beauty.—Yes, Spring, warm, genial Spring is upon us with her sunshine and warm showers, with her green leaves and fresh flowers."

The last week of May marked the end of Ryan's enlistment and, ironically, his transfer from Cahaba to another prison. On May 29 he and his fellow officers boarded the river steamer *Southern Republic* for the voyage up the Alabama River to Montgomery. From the "Cradle of the Confederacy" they moved, closely guarded, by rail "over a very fair and fertile section of country" to Columbus, Georgia. From there, Ryan confided in his diary, "We went to Andersonville, Ga., where our poor men are confined. Andersonville seems to be just equal to no place at all. Our prisoners are confined in a large field without shade or shelter of any kind. I am informed by the Rebel authorities that they now hold about 12,000 of our enlisted men."

Ryan's party fortunately spent only one night at Andersonville, then proceeded northward to Macon, their destination. There, in the old fair grounds roughly a quarter of a mile east of the city, they were deposited in company with 1,200 other captured Union officers. Camp Oglethorpe, as the recently established permanent prison was called, consisted mainly of a three-acre plot surrounded by a high wooden stockade. Around the outside near the top of the stockade ran a parapet on which sentinels were stationed; inside, running parallel at a distance of fifteen feet, was the "dead line," a low picket fence which no prisoner might approach on penalty of being shot. Within the prison enclosure (or "pen") thus established, an ample-sized building provided quarters for generals and other field officers. Captains and lieutenants (who constituted the majority of the prisoners) fared as best they might in the open.[3]

Ryan thought Macon "quite a fine town," but he was not very communicative about Camp Oglethorpe. "We received about the same treatment," he noted simply on June 3, "and about the same amount of rations we have received heretofore in the camps." Thus one has to turn to others for detailed information on such items as food. According to A. C. Roach and Willard Glazier, the rations at Macon consisted mainly of a pint of corn meal daily, two ounces per day of "rancid bacon packed in wood ashes" (in lieu of salt), and, for occasional variation, an ounce of rice or black-eyed peas, plus a half teaspoonful of salt. Lieutenant Roach thought the rations an improvement over those at Libby Prison and Danville; the corn meal, especially, he found preferable to the hard corn bread he had gotten at Libby.[4]

June came, and with it warmer weather. Ryan learned that the prisoners at Macon now numbered 1,450 and that most of them were without shelter, although "arrangements are being made to erect shelts," he reported optimistically. Most of July was hot, but he found (contradictory to the testimony of Glazier and others) that the "health of the prisoners is good."[5]

Although the Confederate government proscribed trading in greenbacks, Ryan soon found that "the Rebel officers and men are quite anxious to exchange their trash for our good money." The rate of exchange was dependent on two factors: supply and the strictness of the prison authorities. At Macon he found that a greenback would bring four and one-half Confederate dollars. Gold was worth "about 20 dollars for one." The price of food was similarly high. Molasses, which the local drummers sold to the prisoners, brought "25 to 35 dollars per gal. in Confed." Flour brought one Confederate dollar a pound, and corn meal ("quite poor at that") sold for from fifty to seventy-five cents per quart.

By late July, 1864, Sherman's advance through Georgia threatened to make Macon untenable, and Confederate authorities set about dispersing the prisoners. On July 28, 600 of them were packed off to Charleston; before daybreak of the following day, Ryan and an equal number were hurried into boxcars for Savannah, Georgia.

Reaching Savannah about six that evening, the prisoners were herded

---

[3] For somewhat colored contemporary descriptions of the Macon prison during this period, see A. C. Roach, *The Prisoner of War and How Treated* (Indianapolis, 1866), and Willard Glazier, *The Capture, the Prison Pen and the Escape* (New York, 1866). Roach and Glazier were fellow prisoners of Ryan at Macon.

[4] See Roach, *Prisoner of War*, p. 130; Glazier, *The Capture*, p. 122. For cooking purposes the prisoners were formed into groups, and each group was provided with a large iron skillet.

[5] Glazier, for example, declared in his diary that "deaths have been very frequent since the warm weather came on." *The Capture*, p. 126.

into a stockaded enclosure bearing the name of Camp Davidson, located
on the edge of the city. The physical arrangements, were similar to those
of the usual Confederate military prison, yet pleasantly different in that
the enclosure was adjacent to the grounds of the city hospital and contained a number of giant, shade-producing oak trees. Likewise, the captives were well treated by the Georgia regulars who served as guards.
Thus could Ryan write on July 31 with satisfaction: "The Confed. authorities issued tents and cooking utensils to the prisoners. Our camp is
a pleasant and shady one. Our rations are of a better quality than any
we have received up to this time."

The prisoners were divided into groups of twenty and a skillet issued
to each group. Each group in turn built brick ovens in which they baked
their corn bread and roasted fresh meat when it was available. The food
was admittedly better than that of most Confederate prisons. But by
now the rigors of nearly seven months of prison life were beginning to
tell on Ryan, though outwardly his health remained good. His entries
for August, 1864, reflected a mixture of discouragement and thankful-
ness:

Here we are [at Savannah] without money, without books, without clothing, and it seems without friends. Thanks be to God, the health of our officers continues good. Out of six hundred confined at this place, only two
have died since we have been here. When I look back and think that I have
had little or no vegetables for the past eight months, I am thankful that
I have not had the scurvy which is very prevalent among the prisoners at
this time.[6]

September brought one of Ryan's infrequent mentions of his captors:

We are still at Savannah, Ga., where we are as well treated as those
in rebellion against a good government are capable of treating prisoners
of war. We receive as much meal and rice as we can use but our ration of
meat is rather small. The health of the officers here is good considering
that this is the sickly season of the South.

At Savannah, as at Macon, the illicit traffic in greenbacks had been
formalized by the prison authorities. There, as Ryan later recalled,
"greenbacks were worth ten for one, but we were only allowed four and
a half for one by the authorities." Likewise at Savannah, as at Macon,
gold was exchanged for Confederate currency at the rate of twenty to
one. Prices in Confederate money of food and other commodities were
in comparable ratio but with an upward allowance for scarcity. "Butter
in Savannah sold for ten dollars per lb," Ryan testified, "onions at the

[6] One of the two deaths was that on Aug. 26 of Capt. W. McGinnis, 74th Illinois.
Ibid., pp. 137, 377.

rate of four small ones for one dollar and Tobacco and everything else in proportion."[7]

Savannah was the best of the prisoner of war camps that Ryan was to encounter; thus it was with mingled apprehension and hope that the prisoners heard the announcement on the evening of September 12, 1864, that they were to evacuate Camp Davidson the following morning. "The Rebels," declared Ryan, "seem to be in a great hurry to get the Federal officers out of Savannah." On hearing the orders, the prisoners raced each other to the skillets in order to convert their corn meal into "pones" to eat on the way to their destination. Because of the limited number of skillets, not a few amusing scenes ensued and the operation consumed the greater part of the night.

Between five and six o'clock in the morning of September 13, 1864, Ryan and the rest of the prisoners caught their last (to some, affectionate) glimpse of Camp Davidson. Outside the stockade they were met by the city militia who guarded them in the streets of Savannah for several hours preparatory to loading them into boxcars for Charleston.

Reaching Charleston that evening, the prisoners were herded to the southeastern part of the city where stood the fortress-like city jail, an impressive (so thought Ryan) octagonal pile of stuccoed masonry surmounted by a forty-foot tower. The building itself served as accommodations for several hundred convicts, Negro prisoners, military offenders, and deserters of both sides. Ryan and his fellow prisoners were crowded instead into the jail yard, an enclosure formed by a high masonry wall linked to the jail building. Here, lacking cooking utensils and amidst what inmates afterwards charged was an impressive array of filth, they dejectedly set about to make their quarters.

Ryan's ire rose; he termed the jail yard "a dirty, filthy place unfit for human beings to live in." Confined in the yard with him, by his count, were approximately 600 Union officers and 300 white and colored Union enlisted men. Unlike some collaborators among the prisoners (who were to join in a Memorial asserting that the Negro captives were actually better off than the white prisoners), his sympathy at once went out to his fellow prisoners of darker hue.

Most of the colored soldiers confined in this prison were captured on Morris or James Co. land about a year ago. These colored soldiers are good loyal men and should be protected by our government. All that these poor fellows receive in the shape of eatables is a small piece of corn bread per

[7] Glazier, who accompanied Ryan to Savannah, reported similar prices: "Flour, four dollars per quart; onions, three for a dollar; potatoes, forty-eight dollars per bushel; bread, two dollars per loaf; butter, ten dollars per pound; eggs, six dollars per dozen; apples, three for a dollar; milk, three dollars per quart." *Ibid.*, p. 131.

day for each man. Most of these are free colored men from the state of Mass.
... The Rebel authorities compel most of our colored troops who fall into
their hands, who were on[c]e slaves, to work on fortifications, plantations
and do other menial service. In other words, they are not treated as prisoners
of war.

Ryan gave no hint that he held any suspicions as to why he was being
kept in Charleston, a city under continuous Union bombardment. What
he may not have known at this time was that he and his fellow officers
were hostages in a preconceived plan to coerce the Federals into a general exchange of officers and enlisted men, to which the Union command
merely replied by placing 600 Confederate officer-prisoners in a stockade on Morris Island in range of the Confederate shore batteries. Hap-
pily, no deaths occurred on either side.[8]

Ryan described his own reaction to the shelling:

We are exposed to the fire of our heavy guns in the rear of Charleston but
as a general thing the Federal prisoners take great delight in seeing and
hearing our shells drop into the heart of this rebellious city. One of the
largest fires which has ever occurred in this city took place here this week,
but the rebs will not acknowledge that it was caused by our shells. This
fire occurred quite close to the jail and during its continuance our batteries
were heard at work shelling that portion of the city which was on fire. The
fragments of two of our shells struck in the jail yard slightly wounding one
of [our] officers.

Ryan's subsequent entries betrayed the extent to which hunger and
discouragement, and now illness, were taking their toll. In the late weeks
of September he reported:

Our rations here are very small, and small as they are, we can scarcely
get wood enough to cook them. The health of our officers is failing very
fast, but the officer in charge of the prison says they cannot be taken to the
hospital as there is no room. My own health is failing fast under the exposure, stench, and miserable fare which is dealt out to us. Medicines of
the right kind seem to be very scarce at this place. Our poor privates who
are confined here have the scurvy so bad and are so weak from sickness
and disease that they are not able to walk.

Those prisoners who could afford to do so augmented their slim rations with food purchased outside the prison, a transaction that was
aided by the rate of exchange. The Charleston Confederates, remarked
Ryan, were "awful anxious to buy greenbacks at $7 and $8 for one in our
money. They would willingly give 25 dollars in Confed for one in gold."

[8] For first-hand accounts of the experiences of the 600 prisoners taken to Morris
Island, see Fritz Fuzzlebug [nee John J. Dunkle], A Brief Narrative of the Miseries
and Sufferings of Six Hundred Confederate Prisoners Sent from Fort Delaware to
Morris' Island to be Punished (Singer's Glen, Va., 1869), and W. H. Morgan, Personal Reminiscences of the War of 1861-65 (Lynchburg, Va., 1911), pp. 231-55.

Second only to food, the prospect of exchange was the all-consuming topic of conversation in Civil War military prisons. The under-provisioned Confederacy hoped to rid itself of the burden and embarrassment of its over-crowded prisoner-of-war pens—and simultaneously to restore its own depleted military ranks—by a general exchange of prisoners. Washington was consistently cool to the suggestion. "We have got to fight until the military power of the South is exhausted," Grant informed Secretary of State Seward, "and if we release or exchange prisoners captured, it simply becomes a war of extermination."

Grant was painfully aware that the enlistments of many of the Union officers and enlisted men in Confederate hands—Ryan being but one example—had expired, whereas the Confederate prisoners, so it was argued, would fight on if released. Ryan, however, appeared to be skeptical of the latter argument. "I have been in over a half dozen prisons in the South and have found nearly every one of them crowded with rebel deserters among whom you will frequently find officers who have deserted the rebel service. . . . As a general thing, these deserters are treated with great severity by the Confederate authorities."[9]

During the week of September 16-23 it rained in Charleston almost every night and the days proved oppressively warm. But on September 23, the lieutenant's morale received an unexpected boost; rumor had it that an agreement had been reached between the two armies for the exchange of prisoners. "Let me say here," was his joyful but guarded response, "that this exchange news is the most joyful intelligence a poor prisoner can hear of. Query, where is Genl. Exchange, or has he been relieved and Genl. Captivity put in his place?" The next day his fortunes soared to the summit; he was told he would leave for Atlanta for exchange the following day.

At 5 A.M. on September 25, Ryan and almost 600 of his fellow captives filed from the Charleston jail yard to the railroad station where, under guard, they entrained for Savannah. The hundred-odd mile trip consumed twelve hours, and Ryan characteristically passed the time in critically surveying the barren landscape. He saw but one tiny hamlet during the entire journey, while he noted that "there is some very fine Rice land but at present it is going to waist."

Reaching Savannah late in the afternoon, the prisoners re-entrained at once for Macon, approximately 190 miles distant. The Georgia countryside through which they passed struck Ryan as equally barren and uninviting, with the result that his sectional pride somewhat rudely mani-

---

[9] Of Federal deserters Ryan earlier wrote: "In this [Charleston] jail the Rebels have in close confinement about one hundred of our deserters who are receiving their just deserts for their cowardice and villainy. As a general thing they are men who are too lazy to work for a living and are too cowardly to fight for the preservation of their country."

fested itself. "Now a man cannot travel six hours in the North without passing by beautiful villages and fine towns, and every few miles one can see small but well cultivated farms. Give me the North with her fine schools and cheap press to the South with her Negro slaves and boasted wealth."

The lieutenant did note with surprise that the railroads between Charleston, Savannah and Macon were "in fair running order and are not badly in want of either engines or cars."

The prisoners reached Macon at noon on September 26 and were taken by their guards to Camp Oglethorpe, where it was revealed that 140 of them would go to Federal-controlled Atlanta on the following day. Ryan was one of the lucky number, and the next morning they were put aboard the Macon and Atlanta Railroad for the sixty-mile ride to Griffin, some forty miles from Atlanta. This was as far as they could travel by rail, explained Ryan, for "the rebels are taking up the tracks from Lovejoy to Griffin." As for the further section from Lovejoy Station to the outskirts of Atlanta, Sherman's army had "utterly destroyed" the tracks.

In his entry of September 28, Ryan triumphantly announced his exchange and his arrival in Atlanta. "I honestly and sincerely believe," he rejoiced, "that this was the happiest moment of my life—Yes, thanks be to God and his good Servant General Sherman, I can once more breathe the free air of heaven."

The rest was anti-climactic. Because of the Confederate interruption of rail communications northward and a bridge washout over the Chattahoochee, Ryan was directed to remain in Atlanta for further orders. He engaged a room at the Trout House, bought some clothing and set about to explore the city. The weather was beautiful, but Atlanta he found not especially attractive; he was astonished, moreover, at the amount of destruction he encountered. "Things," he quickly learned, "are very dear in this town." His room cost him four dollars a day in United States currency; there were no bed clothes and "all they have on the table is a little fresh meat and poor ham, coffee, and molasses." He continued "Yesterday I paid $3.50 [U.S.] for a small three bladed pocket knife of Sheffield make with bone handle. Note paper 50 cts per quire and envelopes (white) 50 cts per pack. I also paid 50 cts for 25 Medallion steel pens, and 15 cts for a common pen holder, and a small bottle of ink was 40 cts. A common ordinary tooth bruth is worth from 75 cts to $1.50 at any sutlers."

On October 3, 1864, Lieutenant Ryan left Atlanta for Marietta, Georgia. There the diary ends. From Marietta, it it known that he proceeded northward until finally he reached Illinois and was mustered out of service at Camp Butler on New Year's Eve, 1864. From there he went to Chicago and set about establishing an insurance business.[10] In the meantime he married. His lungs having been affected by the exposure of his wartime confinements, he contracted tuberculosis which led him in the 1870's to seek relief in Pueblo, Colorado. Ryan died January 29, 1883, in Chicago.

[10] E. E. Ryan and Company, 210 LaSalle Street, established in 1865.

CIVIL WAR HISTORY
A Journal of the Middle Period

A quarterly journal that has been recognized since 1955 as a principal organ of nineteenth-century American history. Originally devoted to an intensive scholarly treatment of the war years, 1861–1865, its scope has broadened to include articles on slavery and abolition, antebellum and Reconstruction politics, diplomacy, and social and cultural developments of the middle period.

In addition to its major articles, a comprehensive book review section in each issue assists the reader in keeping abreast of current literature in the field.

The Civil War remains the pivotal event in American history, and as such its fascination for students, scholars, and the general reader continues unabated. *Civil War History* is the outstanding forum for scholarly studies in this important era.

John T. Hubbell, editor. *Civil War History* is published quarterly by The Kent State University Press, Kent, Ohio 44242.